R. W. Sawtell

The History of the first Baptist Church

For the first seventy Years - from April 22, 1822, to April 22, 1892

R. W. Sawtell

The History of the first Baptist Church
For the first seventy Years - from April 22, 1822, to April 22, 1892

ISBN/EAN: 9783337161682

Printed in Europe, USA, Canada, Australia, Japan

Cover: Foto ©ninafisch / pixelio.de

More available books at **www.hansebooks.com**

OF THE

FIRST BAPTIST CHURCH,

WOODSTOCK, ONT.,

FOR THE FIRST SEVENTY YEARS—FROM
APRIL 22, 1822, TO APRIL 22, 1892.

BY

R. W. SAWTELL.

Printed for the Church by
THE WOODSTOCK TIMES.
1892

PREFACE.

At the monthly business meeting of the church held September 16th, 1891, the following minute occurs: "That Brother R. W. Sawtell be appointed* to write the history of this church." This is the extent of the instructions given—not a word of advice as to length or breadth or scope or plan. No wonder that the matter was never looked into till late in winter; and when it was also well known that others had been previously "appointed" to the work, but had given it up after "looking into it." No wonder, I say, that it was with reluctance that it was ever undertaken by one who had neither experience nor knowledge in "bookmaking." But the fact remained that the church wanted it done and loyalty to the church demanded sacrifice on the part of some one of its members, thus the task was accepted,

The "history" is simply a condensed compilation of the minutes of the Church business and to any but the members and their friends can afford but little pleasure or interest, and for them it is written simply as a book of reference, making no claim to literary merit nor presenting any striking or extraordinary historical events—yet with the writer's conviction that it will be appreciated by the present and future members of the Church as a memento of the doings of those who have gone before and are now enjoying the fruits of their labors in the "Better Land."

INTRODUCTION.

Few churches of any denomination possess records the publication of which would excite interest outside its own memberbership and adherents. Some have been, published and failed even to interest its own members. Among the few which have created more than ordinary notice "The Broadmead Records" may be mentioned. This was the history of an old Baptist Church at Bristol, England, existing since the year 1640, and which had the distinction of furnishing victims deemed worthy of persecution and imprisonment, if not for the stake, for opinions held and maintained in favor of soul-liberty, and who willingly suffered tortures in defence of the truth.

The First Baptist Church of Oxford possesses no such striking records, hence can claim no such distinction, neither can we hope to create an interest outside our own circle and friends. Probably not one in a hundred of our present or past membership have examined our records and few of our younger members have a true conception of the origin and past history of the Church. It has been thought wise by the Church that for this reason, and also on account of the fast fading manuscript, to endeavor to rescue at least the leading events of the past 70 years and place them within the reach of every member in a condensed and readable form, and thus, at least, to preserve the facts, and if such should excite an interest and a determination on the part of our members to become better acquainted with the history of their own denomination at large a greater point will have been gained.

If it were allowable to interweave matters which suggest

themselves to our minds as we peruse the records, it would not
be difficult to create an interest beyond our little circle or even
the boundaries of our county. The period of the existence of
our church would embrace the dawn of settlement and civiliz-
ation of western Canada as well as the history of the wonderful strides in agriculture, education, and the arts and sciences of
the nineteenth century.

It would show the progress of agriculture from the stripping
of the dense forests of timber through which the red men had
roamed for centuries unmolested by their white brothers and
the development of the soil into the beautifully cultured farms
which we witness today: it would exhibit the progress of archi-
tecture from the bark covered shanty of the early settler, built
by the use of the axe alone, to the costly residences, commercial
palaces, churches and public buildings, culminating in the mag-
nificent structure now nearing completion for our county courts
and public offices ; it would array before our eyes the tools and
implements, as some of us have seen them, in advancing usefulness in every decade, from the sickle and cradle to the almost
perfect machinery of the day and with which our farmers are
familiar. It would remind us also that the use of steam as a
motive power was scarcely known, and very little of the
machinery which is now through its discovery brought into use ;
that railroads were then unknown and steam boats almost
equally unused : that electricity has been harnessed, not only
for telegraphing and lighting, but for locomotive and motor
power in every conceivable form. The indispensable telephone,
the phonograph, the typewriter, and a thousand other useful
and ornamental articles owe their discoveries to the period
mentioned.

Then, too, the origin and perfection of our public school
system, with our advanced colleges of learning, our public anp

free libraries, our various benevolent and charitable institutions and hospitals have, in this short period, attained to considerable eminence.

When we think of the picture of loneliness presented by a solitary shanty in the dense wilderness and perchance not even the sound of any other axe within hearing, or a friend within many miles, we might well say that "the pioneers of that day were worthy of being classed as heroes of great courage and determination."

The earliest record that we have of the settlement of this county dates back almost a century. In the year 1793 Col. Simcoe, then Governor of Canada, invited the U. E. Loyalists who had manifested by acts of daring and courage their love for the British flag and a desire for its maintenance, to come into Canada and possess the land.

The first who responded to his invitation was Thomas Horner, who came and pitched his tent in Blenheim, on the banks of the stream now known as Horner's Creek. The Governor had three concessions surveyed and presented to him. Mr. Horner subsequently moved his family there and began a settlement by building a saw mill the materials for which had to be carted all the way from York State. The next settler, as far as we know, was Thomas Ingersoll who selected "Oxford on the Thames," which consisted of what is now known as three townships by the name of Oxford East, West and North. Mr. Ingersoll settled on the banks of the Thames where Ingersoll now stands, which was named after him.

Unfortunately both these gentlemen, after they had spent much labor and some money in surveying and making roads, lost nearly all the lands given them by Governor Simcoe, they being escheated to the Crown. It was discovered after the governor was recalled and his successor came that no patent had been issued and the then government ignored their just claims except a small position to which they were entitled as squatters.

Subsequently Benjamin Loomis settled in West Oxford and Peter Lossing in Norwich, where he founded the colony of quakers and to which place many followed him.

The assessment roll for 1812 contains 64 names only and out of which the following in the nearest settlement are selected, viz: Veron Mather, lot 12, E. Oxford, 200 acres, 12 cleared, 1 horse, 2 cows : Robert Clarke, lot 13, 200 acres, 18 cleared, 2 horses, 2 oxen, 2 cows ; Levi Luddington, lot 17, 200 acres, 20 cleared, 1 horse, 2 oxen, 4 cows; Zecharia Burtch, lot 18, 200 acres, 30 cleared, 1 horse, 2 oxen, 4 cows; Archibald Burtch, lot 19, 100 acres, 6 cleared, 1 horse, 1 cow; Levi Babbit, lot 20, 100 acres 14 cleared, 1 horse, 1 cow.

In 1817 the population of the whole county (which then in included west Nissouri, Burford and Oakland townships) had increased to 530 with 78 houses so called, 1 minister, Elder Maybee in West Oxford, presiding over a strict communion Baptist church, but no place of worship ; one grist mill two saw mills, but no school, no police court and no gaol.

Among the very early settlers we find the names of those who became constituent members of this church and others who joined soon after, nearly all of whom were U. E. Loyalists.

Old Country emigrants had not yet reached this far inland, hence New England customs and New England religion were largely adopted.

In the fall of 1821 Elder Tallman, an open communion Baptist, came into this county for the purpose of settling his son on some land in Zorra. He did not wish it to be known that he was a preacher, but it inadvertantly leaked out and he could not resist the demand for a sermon, and after hearing one they wanted more. It soon spread over the settlement and they

flocked for miles to hear him. He seemed to have been a man
of considerable force and influence and soon gathered a following.   He returned to his home in York State before winter,
leaving his son in Canada.

At this time there were about 2,000 inhabitants in the
county where there are now nearly 50,000, and then but 1,000
in "Little Muddy York," where there are now nearly 200,000
in the great metropolis of the Province of Ontario—Toronto.

In the spring of 1822 Elder Tallman returned to Oxford,
whether by invitation of his admirers here or to see what his
son was doing, or his own desire as an evangelist it is not said,
but the result of his visit was the formation of an open communion Baptist Church. The first and for ten years the only
church in the settlement where Woodstock now stands.

CHAPTER I.

ELDER TALLMAN-CONSTITUENT MEMBERS —ORGANIZATION -FIRST BAP-
TISM—ADOPTION OF A COVENANT AND RULES OF FAITH—BAPTISM
IN HORNER'S CREEK—CHURCH FORMED IN BLENHEIM - ORDIN-
ATION OF ELDERS CROSS AND HARRIS--SPRINGFORD CHURCH—THE
FIRST CONVENTION—A. BURTCH—W. H. LANDON.

In the year of our Lord one thousand eight hundred and
twenty two Elder Thomas Tallman, pastor of the First Free
Communion Baptist church of Worchester, Sharon and Cobuskill,
State of New York, made a visit to this part of Canada, duly
authorised to constitute and organize churches wherever God
in His Providence may cast his lot and proper applications being
made to him for that purpose.

There can be no doubt as to the authority delegated to him,
and it is also evident that he was a man of persuasive and mag-
netic power, for we learn that the persons whose names constitute "The First Free Communion Baptist Church in the Town
of Oxford" had been members of the "Close Communion Church
in Oxford." The following are the names:—

Salmon King, Rufus Foster, John B. Tree, Richard Tims,
Horace Cross, Mathew Randall, David Cross, jr, Ira Barr,
Lois Dibble, Elizabeth Welch, Elizabeth Tree, Lydia Sickles,
Lucy Barr, Charity King, Rebecca Randall, Rachel Thornton,
Betsy Cross, Lydia King, Abigal Foster."

The petition to Elder Tallman to constitute and organise the
foregoing parties into a church to be called "The First Free
Communion Baptist Church of the Town of Oxford," was duly
presented and notice given for such purpose to take place at the
school house. The following is the record: --

"Oxford, April 22nd, 1822, met agreeable to previous notice,
on the Governor's Road at the school house near Bro. Tree's and
made application to Elder Tallman, who called on Bro. Cross
and Bro. Welch to sit in council with him and it was their

opinion that each member should give a relation of the work of
God's grace on their hearts and the travel of their minds touch-
ing the present application which was individually complied
with, and after which he proceeded to constitute and organiz-
the church in gospel order and rule. After which came forward Brothers V. Welch and D. Cross and joined the church,
and the brethren gave Bro. Cross liberty to improve his gifts
in holding meetings and expounding the Scriptures wherever
God in His providence may open a door." (Sgd) Salmon King,
ch. clk.

At the same meeting, Joseph Northrip and John Baldwin
told their experience, were baptized and received the hand of
fellowship, thus constituting a church of twenty-one members. A covenant and rules of faith, almost as long as
the 39 articles, were adopted and subscribed to by
every member. One article provided for the setting
apart one day in every month to acknowledge their covenant.
Thus began that, to them, all important meeting which seemed
to constitute the test of true discipleship and firm adherence to
the cause. For a period of forty years these monthly week day
meetings were held with more or less regularity and enthusiasm,
but were long since replaced by the weekly prayer meeting,
where the edification of each other by the relation of Christian
experience was continued, but the practice of exclusion for
failing to confess orally to the covenant and articles of faith
was discontinued. Another article provided for discipline of
members by the vote of "male members only." It would be interesting to reproduce the whole but space forbids.

April 29. The church met at the school house near Bro.
Cross', agreeable to notice, "to receive a number of members
which could not attend last Saturday, when Elder Tallman
preached. On the following Sunday they were baptized and
received the hand of fellowship, after which the communion of
the Lord's supper was celebrated."

At every monthly meeting additions were made to this infant
cause and the Spirit of Christ was manifest in the conversion of
souls. At the June meeting Elders Bangford and Tallman
preached. James Harris (after preaching on the following Sun-

day) was "received into fellowship and granted a license to improve his gifts."

On the 13th of October "A general meeting" was held near Horner's Creek, in Blenheim, at the house of Joseph Smith, Elder Tallman preached, after which eight were baptized in Horner's Creek. A church was then formed consisting of thirteen members. J. Goble was elected to serve as deacon and Bro. Slaughson, clerk. Richard Tims was the first deacon elected to serve the Oxford church.

On the 31st of the same month we learn that "a council was held in the house of David Curtis for the purpose of ordaining Darius Cross and James Harris." The delegates from the Oxchurch were Elder Tallman. L. H. Perry, Vine Welch, J. B. Tree and Salmon King. Elder Tallman was moderator and S. King. clerk. At the November covenant meeting the first case of discipline (The cause being excessive drinking) was carried to the exclusion of the member.

Among the additions for the year of its organization we find the familiar names of Abigail Burtch, Laura Harris, N. Hill, J. Vanduzen and Joseph S. Sickles

On the 25th of January, 1823, the question of finance was discussed, apparently for the first time, and it has been a live and important question all through its history. On that occasion the conclusion reached was embodied in this resolve: "That each male member shall pay six cents per month for the necessary expenses of the church and that Salmon King be the treasurer to receive the said tax." There are two points worthy of notice here, viz: "That Canada Currency" was not then in common use and that church finances were not characterized by voluntaryism. The next item worthy of note occurs March 29th, 1823, when, after the covenant meeting it was "voted that an address be sent to the free communion Baptist conference, to be held at Bowman's Creek next June, and a day to be set apart for fasting and prayer the second Thursday in May. This was the first effort to seek recognition by the body to which the church had attached itself.

At the covenant meeting April 26th, John Smith from the States was received by experience and letters of recommendation and was licensed to improve his gifts.

During the year 1823 we find that Elders Tallman, Cross
and Harris made frequent visits to the lower settlement—as
South Norwich was then called—and preached acceptably and
the result was that in February, 1824, "the brethren there asked
to be set apart as a branch church." This appears to have been
done after the general conference and what is now known as the
Springford church was duly constituted.

Among the many familiar names of persons admitted in 1824
we find those of Sprague, Dibble, Aldrich, Dean, Luddington,
Clark, Lamport, Hallock and Burtch. The last named was
baptized on the 28th day of August and in December following
he was appointed deacon, and L. H. Perry church clerk.

On January the 16th, 1825, a meeting was held in Taft's
school house in Zorra—or over the river as it was called—when
A. Taft and wife, E. Cody and wife, M. Cody and E. McQuain
were baptized. On the following June we find that A. Taft
was appointed deacon and Darius Cross clerk of that branch
of the church in Zorra.

Among the papers preserved are the original minutes of
"The Free Communion Baptist Association of Upper Canada,
in convention at the house of Deacon Archibald Burtch in East
Oxford, on the 24th of June, 1825," at which Elder Goble
preached and Elders Cross and Harris and many others felt
the "freedom of the Spirit and spoke of the goodness of God."

Elder Goble was chosen moderator, and L. H. Perry, clerk of
the conference, then proceeded to read the letters of the
churches, when the following statistics were given, viz.: Blenheim church 37 members ; Southold 15 ; Oxford 79; Norwich
15 ; total 146. A petition from the Norwich branch was read
"asking to be set apart as a church." Petition granted and
the hand of fellowship given by the moderator.

After completing the business of the conference it was "voted
that the clerk prepare the minutes for the press and have them
printed."

On the 30th of July a covenant meeting was held at Harris
Street, for the purpose of settling some difficulty among the
brethren, the nature of which is indistinguishable in the fading
record, but some exclusions took place : the frequency of which
in those early days indicate that either a laxness in the ad-

mission of members or a puritanical strictness in discipline existed.

The years 1824 and 1825 witnessed large accessions, numbering not less than 42, mostly by baptism. Among them were members of families whose descendants remain with us, viz: Hallock, Rowell, Dolson, Lamport, Burtch and Gee, not forgetting one who more than any other in after years taught and served the church in its various struggles and prosperities for nearly twenty five years, we refer to William Henry Landon. He was admitted by letter on the 30th of December, 1825. About the same period Jane Blow, who had been baptized by Elder Cross and joined the church in Blenheim, subsequently coming to Woodstock and becoming a member where she has to this, its seventieth anniversary, wielded a great influence by her walk, conversation and example as the honored wife and widow of Deacon Burtch.

At the January meeting 1826, several cases of discipline were dealt with and exclusions followed in great solemnity. At the same meeting Deacon A. Burtch was chosen church clerk protem. By the close of this year the number of members had reached the comparatively large aggregate of eighty. The covenant meetings had been variously well attended either at Taft's school house, at Harris street in West Oxford, in the Rowell settlement in East Zorra, or at head quarters—Governor's Road—as the place where Woodstock now stands was then called. While they seemed to have had no paid pastor the church was supplied and the ordinances administered by Elder Tallman, then Elder Cross, while Elders Harris and Goble frequently preached. The first church worshipped in the log school house on the corner of what is now Dundas and Chapel streets, and when the congregation was large in Deacon Burtch's barn. In 1827 no additions were made and only two in 1828. On the 30th of August of this year W. H. Landon was duly ordained an elder, and thence forward devoted much of his time and talent to the interests of the church.

CHAPTER II.

The year 1829 seemed to have been a year of great zeal and
large accessions. Among the first baptized we find the names
of George and Hannah Blake, Anna Welch, Henry and Lucy
Lamport. Later in the year, Stephen B. Tree, Thomas Earl,
Elijah Hill, Benjamin Lamport, Edward Topping and many
others, numbering forty-two, whose names are still familiar to
us and many of whom the older members were well acquainted
with. Jeremia Letts, one of the 42 mentioned, was shortly after
made church clerk, but some trouble having arisen he resigned
till it should be cleared up and Deacon Burtch again assumed
the duties.

On the 12th, 13th and 14th of June 1829, the "Eighth
annual Free Communion Baptist conference of Upper Canada"
was held in the house of Deacon Burtch. A copy of the minutes
has been preserved which states "That Elder David Marks
preached the introductory discourse from 1 Peter 2-5 verses."

David Marks in his autobiography refers to this occasion and
says: "The Lord favored me with one of my best seasons and
comforted the hearts of many." He goes on to say "our yearly
meeting had appointed Bro. Straight and myself to attend this
conference, to open a correspondence and labor to effect a union
with this people. They received us affectionately and advised
their churches to appoint messengers to meet in conference with
us in two weeks."

This conference seems to have been a very pleasant one.
Elder Landon was elected Moderator and Oran Wright, Clerk.
The number reported as members of the Oxford Church was 69.
Elder Marks, as nearly all know, was an evangelist whose labors

in the interest of the "Free-will Baptist Church of America" were remarkable. He made several tours through this part of Canada, preaching to large assemblies who gathered from great distances to near him. In the same year (September 20, 1829), he married Marrilla Turner, a daughter of Capt. Turner, then residing on the Governor's road, on the 1st lot of the 10th concession of Zorra. He speaks very highly of the reception he always got from the Baptists of Oxford, and was anxious to bring about the church union referred to.

We learn, from his work, that the joint meeting was held at Oxford the last of June, when there were present six delegates from the "Free-will Baptists" and fourteen from the Free Communion Baptists." After fully discussing the subject of union, they found that the chief differences between them were : " Whereas the Free-will Baptists maintain that a saint, in this state of probation, may lose that grace and that character which constitute him such, and thus finally perish : the Free Communion Baptists generally maintain the reverse. Secondly : That Free Communion Baptists have a few written articles of faith, abstract from the Scriptures, while the Free-will Baptists acknowledge no standard but the Bible."

It was agreed to meet at the Holland Purchase yearly meeting in August and endeavor to effect a union.

Elder Harris attended the meeting, but there is no evidence that a union such as Elder Marks desired was ever formed.

On the 30th day of May, 1830, the following were appointed delegates to the general conference, viz.: Elders J. Harris and J. Goble, brethren A. Burtch, S. Rowell, M. Cody, E. Cross and E. Topping. It is not stated where the conference was held this year.

At the covenant meeting, held at the school-house, July 31, 1830, Bro. Coulburn asked for a "letter of recommendation from the church." On being asked why ? he replied : "That, being a public speaker, he could not conscientiously preach final perseverence." The church "voted he should have a letter, but not of recommendation ; for he brought occasions against the church." Thus, in the past, as well as the present, men differed in doctrinal belief and discussed their differences ; but, like Paul and Barnabas, parted company.

On the 28th of August it was voted "that at the next covenant meeting there be a donation by the brethren to defray the
expenses of printing our minutes." This, certainly, was an evidence of progression ; also, that there were facilities, within
their reach, for preserving a record of their doings through the
press.

We learn that a council was called, to meet at the Blenheim
Church on the 30th of October, to settle some difficulty, which
had arisen in that infant church, and the following large dele-
gation was sent from the parent church : Elders Cross and
Harris, Brethren Burtch, Rowell, Blake, Letts, Rexford, Perry,
Topping, B. Lamport, H. Lamport, J. Barraclif, S. B. Tree, N.
Brown and D. Burtch.

Reuben Martin was appointed Church Clerk, December 3.
At the same meeting a resolution was passed to "set off East
Zorra Church as a branch of the Oxford Church."

Elder Tallman, whose absence is not accounted for, again appears at the covenant meeting in October, and subsequent meetings to May, 1831, when he, with Elders Cross and Harris, and
Brethren A. Burtch and R. Martin were appointed delegates to
the general conference to be held the 10th day of June.

A very interesting covenant meeting was held October 29th
in which Elder Jenkins, Elder Landon and a large number of
members took part ; and also a number of candidates gave their
experience and applied for baptism.

The brethren at Harris street made a request to the Oxford
Church, on the 10th of December, 1831, to be set off as a sepa-
rate cause, to be called "the second branch of Oxford Church."

At the covenant meeting, August 25th, 1832, we find that a
license was granted to Brother E. Topping "to improve his
gifts, wherever God in His Providence may call him." There
were then 82 members in good standing. In February, 1833,
Jeremiah Letts was again appointed church clerk. There is no
other record for that year.

For 1834-5 there is no record, and until October, 1836, there
seems to have been a barren, unfruitful period. Covenant meetings were occasionally held for discipline, but no evidence is
given of stated preaching. At this time, however, there was " a
manifest disposition to return to the Lord, from whom they had
wandered."

A frame chapel was erected, and opened on the 27th day of December, 1836. Elder Landon preached the dedication sermon, from Psalm 27, verse 4. The meetings were continued eleven days, and "the Lord poured out His spirit in a wonderful manner—saints were revived and souls converted."

January 1st, 1837, a large number were baptised, including the names of W. and E. Favey, Julius Perry, James, Jacob and Mary Topping, Mary Perry, D. Luddington and others.

At the covenant meeting January 28th, 1837, Almon Tree and Huldah Tree presented letters from Rushford and Lyndon, N. York, and Belinda Landon, T. Mathews, Chester Withy, Pamelia Luddington and Frances Waterbury received the hand of fellowship; and at the close of the meeting it was voted : "That five dollars shall be paid out of the common funds of the church to Master Henry Burtch ; upon the condition that he make all the necessary fires, in proper season, for all the meetings of the church, and keeping the house swept, until the first of January, 1838."

The record fails to tell if the money was paid or the conditions complied with. Nor does it say that the rebellion of that year interfered with the fulfillment of the duties. The party named has no recollection of spending the stipend mentioned, hence it is unlikely that he carried out the contract.

February 25, 1837, R. H. Burtch and Elijah Tree were baptised by elder Landon. James Guild and William Burtch, March 3rd.

At the April covenant meeting, a resolution was passed to "make a subscription for the temporal support of Elder Landon for the coming year."

August 28th an effort was made with the Eastern Baptist Association to hold a general convention of Baptists at Townsend, to meet the third Wednesday in September. Elder Landon and Deacon Burtch to be delegates, with authority to "support an association, without infringing on the rights of individual churches." Here we observe the indication of sturdy, Baptist independence.

E. Topping and Philip Mitchell were appointed deacons on the 30th of Sept.

There is no record for 1839.

May 30th, 1840, E. Topping, A. Burtch, G. Blake, J. Letts and Elder Landon were elected delegates to the association to be held at Waterford.

On the 25th of July the delegation reported to the church in favor of withdrawal from the association, which was accordingly done, but no reason is assigned for such withdrawal.

May 30th, 1841, Elder Landon was appointed a delegate to Haldimand for the purpose of "meeting the ministers of the denomination," and August the 27th it was ordered that a collection be taken up next day to defray the expenses of said delegate. At the same meeting R. H. Burtch was elected church clerk and in the month of October treasurer also.

Sept. 25th, 1841, it was "voted that there be no invitations on communion occasions hereafter, until a final adjustment of the question."

On the 29th of January, 1842, it was moved by G. Blake, seconded by A. Burtch, That the communion question be settled—that the communion be restricted to baptised believers" carried without a dissenting voice. Thus a question which no doubt had led to many dissentions and frequent discussions was unanimously set at rest and the church came more into harmony with the practice of the regular Baptist churches of the Province, now rapidly increasing.

CHAPTER III.

Elder Landon Resigned—Call to Rev. Mr. Bosworth—Short
Pastorate—Objections to Women Speaking in Public—His
Resignation—A Call to Elder Landon not Accepted—Elder
Topping Accepted a Call to the Pastorate—His Resignation.

Elder Landon, whose connection with the church had been
long and profitable, resigned July 31st, 1842. It was then resolved to extend a call to the Rev. Mr. Bosworth. The call
was accepted and he became the pastor of the church. Rev.
Mr. Landon shortly after applied for a letter which was granted.

Feb. 25, 1843, Rev. Mr. Bosworth and wife presented their
letters and were received. At the same meeting an application
was made by letter by the Brantford church for assistance in
money, but no action was taken. It appears that even in the
"good old days of yore" churches were not entirely free from
some of the evils so prevalent at the present time.

At the April business meeting in 1844 we learn that the
Rev. N. Bosworth "gave a statement of the pecuniary affairs of
the church," when it was agreed that the "Deacons collect subscriptions."

August 31st, 1844, Elizabeth Laycock was admitted as a candidate for baptism. At a subsequent meeting brethren John
Muir, T. Letts, W. Pavey, A. Burtch and P. Mitchell were appointed a committee to visit delinquent members and cite them
to the first covenant meeting.

This same matter has always been a trouble to the church
officers throughout its history and we may be sure that it is not
peculiar to this church. But in the early days we learn that
the covenant meeting was looked upon as the true test of
discipleship. One might absent himself from the communion
on Sabbath and nothing said, but if absent from the covenant

meeting twice in succession he was at once cited to appear at the next, and if he could not give a sufficient reason for absence he was warned that he would be labored with, and many were excluded for non-attendance. Others who attended and failed to "acknowlege their covenant," were likewise dealt with.

At the monthly meeting held November 30th it was agreed that a prayer meeting be held at the house of Deacon Burtch " for the prosperity of the church."

The following monthly meeting was one of more than usual interest. The pastor, Mr. Bosworth, stated that from an examination of the Scriptures, it was his opinion that it was not scriptural for females to speak in public meetings, therefore, he felt it his duty on account of his difference of opinion with the church to tender his resignation as pastor. He left with the statement that "he would return to the meeting if required."

The Rev. E. Topping was at once called to the chair—

When it was moved by G. Blake seconded by J. Muir "That both males and females give their opinion on the subject." A lengthened discussion took place resulting in resolutions being passed as follows :

Resolved 1st "That we cannot perceive passages of Scripture in the Bible to prohibit females from speaking and praying in common with the males in public meetings."

Resolved 2nd "That we respectfully receive the resignation of Mr. Bosworth as pastor of this church, but cordially invite him to preach for us as long as he is at liberty or until the church can obtain another pastor—pledging ourselves to contribute as formerly."—Carried by a large majority.

At the monthly meeting in May the Rev. N. Bosworth applied for letters of dismission for himself and wife which were granted.

Thus ended a two years' pastorate of a man whom we are assured was a scholar and a gentleman, as well as a pious and eloquent preacher. His cultured and student habits seemed to have unfitted him for the rural, uncultured state of society, which necessarily existed at that early period. It is natural to sup-

pose that a people accustomed to the burning and stirring but
homely and practical preaching of such evangelists as Tallman,
Cross, Harris, Marks, and Landon, could not so readily appreci-
ate the highly cultured and scholastic learning as it is said this
pastor manifested in his discourses.

It is true that Mr. Landon had, in a measure, introduced
a style of preaching both learned and exalting, acquired by
diligent self culture and intense study, but Mr. Bosworth seemed
to have been in advance of the environment of the times and
circumstances which he had fallen into in this new world.

On the 31st of May, 1845, "a unanimous call" was tendered
to Rev. W. H. Landon, to again become the pastor of the
church, but it was not accepted.

Deacon Letts and wife who were among the very earliest
settlers of Zorra as well as members of this church received
letters of dismission, Aug. 25th, on their leaving this country
for the States.

A committee was appointed to procure a pastor, and on
the 27th of December, they reported "That as the Rev. E.
Topping had officiated as pastor for about nine months he be
now called to the pastoral care of the church." No objections
were raised. On the following day Mr. Topping accepted the
charge.

This union only continued till the August meeting, 1846,
when we find that "the Rev. E. Topping resigned the pastoral
care of the church."

At the September meeting a resolution was unanimously
passed, again calling the Rev. Mr. Landon to assume the duties
of pastor.

On the 30th of January, 1847, it was agreed that a tea meeting should be held in the chapel on the 25th of February and
the proceeds thereof applied to repairing the chapel, Rev. Mr.
Landon, M. L. Green, Geo. Midgley and R. H. Bartch to be the
committee of management and subsequently "spend the money
as they think proper on the chapel."

On the 28th of March another advance step was taken, viz:

"That the seats be alloted and the persons choosing a seat pay
what they think proper for one year,"

Bro. John Hatch and C. C. Carryer were baptized April 25th
and received the hand of fellowship as members of the church.

An adjourned church meeting was held on the 14th of October,
1847, when a series of resolutions was passed having reference
to the progress and welfare of the church, and among them was
one to appoint a sexton permanently and empower him to charge
10 shillings for digging each grave, retaining 7s. 6 pence for his
own services and paying the balance to the treasurer to form a
fund to keep the grounds in repair; "That a collection be
taken up every Sabbath for contingent expenses;" "That this
church cannot consider any person a member of it who does not
under ordinary circumstances meet with it at least every
Sabbath."

The burying ground was on an opposite lot on the west side
of Chapel street as well as on the chapel lot.

CHAPTER IV.

DISCOURAGING TIMES—REORGANIZATION—ELDER LANDON AGAIN RE-
SIGNS—ELDER WINTERBOTHAM—REGULAR BAPTIST PRINCIPLES—
GRAND RIVER ASSOCIATION - CLERGY RESERVES - ELDER WINTER-
BOTHAM RESIGNS.

It is evident from the experience of this church, and probably
of all others, that members cannot be made pious, prayerful, or
live consistent christians by passing resolutions at church meetings any more than by act of parliament.

"As it was in the beginning is now and ever shall be," unless
the grace of God reigns in the heart religious efforts and
christian duties will simply be perfunctionary and spasmodic.

Love for Christ and obedience to His commands, deeply rooted in the heart, will result in perseverance and constancy when all else fail.

Such was found to be the case in this church, and to such an extent at this period we find that practically a new organization took place in the beginning of the year 1848, when a new covenant was entered into and only those pledging themselves to faithfully adhere to its provisions were invited or permitted to subscribe to it. The provision of the articles and covenant were such as the church by their experience had then attained to and to which the following names were subscribed at this meeting, the 27th of January, 1848, viz:—A. Burtch, Deacon, Daniel Burtch, J. Hatch, R. Martin, H. Dibble, G. Blake, (Deacon), J. McColl, C. Baguley, Ann Jackman, Elizabeth Thompson, John McColl, N. Bartley, D. Thompson, Jane Burtch, E. Landon, E. Laycock, Janet Hay, Mary Mitchell, Mary Barnes, James Guild, Laura Burtch, Hannah Blake, M. A. Hatch, C. C. Carryer.

By the end of the year the number reached thirty—28 of the former members, one by baptism and one by letter.

Mr. Landon again tendered his resignation in January, 1849, but was induced to remain. The church appears to have had severe struggles at this period. The matter of finance was repeatedly up for discussion. In September of that year we find a series of resolutions and urgent appeals to the little band for help, and at the same time urging Mr. Landon to remain as their pastor.

From the last date to the 4th of May, 1851, there is no record; but at this meeting we learn that Messrs. Winterbotham, A. Burtch and James Martin were appointed a committee "to draft a letter of application and an epitome of our principles, preparatory to their being presented to the Grand River Association to be laid before the next church meeting." (Sgd.) James Martin, assistant church clerk.

Thus the new pastor, Elder Winterbotham, and the new clerk, John Hatch, and assistant clerk James Martin, are suddenly introduced without a record of how or when, but the fact was already being felt and the influence of the sturdy old Baptist pastor is manifest in the letter prepared and presented for the church's adoption at a meeting held May 31st, 1851.

It would be interesting to copy the whole document but a few points of information must suffice. (1) "We hold the sacred Scriptures to be the only rule of faith and practice." (2) We only commune in the Lord's supper with those who have been immersed in the divine name, who give evidence of regeneration by walking in newness of life. We require unanimity in receiving persons to fellowship and in all acts of church discipline, such as public rebuke and exclusion. (3) We have enjoyed peace and steady progress since the reorganization of the church on regular Baptist principles on the 2nd day of January, 1848. Our number now is sixty-six." (4) "We have a Sabbath school, Bible class and auxilliary missionary society for the benefit of the inhabitants of the town." This lengthy document was dated 31st of May, 1851, and the following delegates appointed to present it to the "Grand River Association," viz: Pastor Winterbotham, Deacons Burtch and Blake and Brethren J. Martin, L. Green, J. Hatch, R. Kipp, J. Goble, J. Hoile, R. H. Burtch and M. Green with power to withold the letter should circumstances dictate."

It seems that such circumstances did arise, for we find that a committee was appointed by the association to meet a committee from the church to discuss some vital question at issue.

The committee appointed by the church at a subsequent meeting was the Pastor, Deacon Goble, Hatch, Martin and Hoile, and it was decided to hold a public meeting in the evening.

Aug. 31st, 1851, it was resolved "That the printed circular from Toronto purporting to call a meeting at Hamilton on the first Wednesday in October next, in support of the course of religious equality be approved, and Mr. Winterbotham return an answer accordingly.

At a church meeting held on the 4th of October, 1851, it was moved by Brother McColl, seconded by Brother Blake, "That the statement of the stand taken by the church, in reference to the matters at issue between it and the association, be published in The Observer.

A lengthy document is here inserted in the minutes, which sets forth the discussion and decision of the committee of the association, which decided, by three to two, against the reception of the church into the association. The only objection seems to be that the association held that the ordinances of the church should only be administered, in any case, by one who had been regularly ordained, by other ministers also regularly ordained. The church held that this rule, while desirable, was not always practicable; and decided that no amended application should be made to the association.

Among the additions mentioned here are those of Mr. and Mrs. Vincent, dismissed by letter from the Peterborough Church.

Resolutions were passed to raise the pastor's salary $50 for the ensuing year—but no mention is made of the total sum. (2). To take up subscriptions to liquidate the debt incurred for incidental expenses. (3). To take steps to erect a shed for protecting the horses.

The year 1852 began with the purchase of a new pulpit Bible from George Barnes, at the price of 22s 6d.

At the February meeting Robert and Mary Barbour were admitted, on condition "that they receive their letters from Montreal." William Winter and wife and daughter Mary were received by letter from the Pickering Church. At the following monthly meeting it was:

Resolved, "That Bro. W. Winter sustain his former office, and be acknowledged as a deacon of this church."

On July 31st Mr. Winterbotham was authorised to obtain a minister, during the ensuing month, to preach a sermon and take up a collection for the benefit of the colored church in the Town of Woodstock."

That Bro. H. Ford be appointed to the Burford station, to preach as often as convenient. That Mr. Winterbotham be requested to continue the pastoral charge another year, from the 20th of September.

On the 28th day of August the following very suggestive resolution was passed :

Resolved, "That whereas the appearance of the small interest the government is taking in the all important questions of the Clergy Reserves and religious state endowments, we consider it our duty, at the present juncture, to call the attention of parliament to the same by petition ; and we do hereby authorize our Pastor and Deacons to make out and sign the same in our behalf, as a church, and forward it without delay."

January 29th, 1853, E. Topping was received by letter, Mrs. Topping by profession, and R. W. Sawtell as a candidate for baptism—on the following day. The next few meetings witnessed large accessions by baptism and profession, and the first indication of preparation for erecting a new church was at the May meeting, when a "site committee" was appointed, consisting of the trustees and Deacon Winter "

This, also, is the first mention of trustees, and the names are not given

July 30th we find the following resolution recorded :

Resolved, That we receive Mr. Winterbotham's resignation with regret on our part, and sorrowful sympathy for such a step on his part," etc. It is gathered from the lengthy resolution that some affliction of great sadness had been experienced, which necessitated his removal, and which the church very much regretted.

A committee consisting of Mr. Landon, Deacons Winter, Goble, Burtch and Martin, were named to look for a successor to Mr. Winterbotham.

"Messrs. Winterbotham, Topping and Winter to be delegates to the convention, to be held at Burford on the first of September ; and a prayer meeting be held for said purpose."

The following resolutions were passed at the next few meetings in the year, viz.: " That we pay each preacher for a Sabbath sermon one pound " ; " That Messrs. Landon, Topping, Burtch, Winter and Martin be a committee to supply the pulpit till we get a pastor " ; " That C. C. Carryer be clerk of the pecuniary affairs of the church " ; "That this church consider it necessary that steps be forthwith taken to erect a new chapel for public worship." The committee appointed to procure plans and carry on this work was composed as follows :—W. H. Landon, Deacons Winter, Hatch and Martin, and J. McColl, C. C. Carryer and R. Barbour.

At the first meeting held in 1854, January 10th, the determination to build was confirmed and a committee appointed to procure subscriptions ; " that they be paid in four instalments; and when £700 shall have been subscribed, the committee to proceed with the erection of the building." A heading for the list was drawn up and then approved.

Mr Landon was authorised, at the next church meeting, to write to Elder Dempsey at St. Andrews, with a view to a call to him as pastor.

At this meeting the site committee reported that they had examined several lots and preferred the one on the corner of Beale and Adelaide streets ; but then it was not in the market. They would not recommend any less than 75 feet frontage, and that a corner lot, also.

March 25th it was resolved to appropriate the communion collections to a poor fund.

There seems to have been a question as to removal from the old site on Chapel street, and it was decided to meet on the 5th of April and ballot for a decision. Mrs. Landon and Mrs. H. T. Burtch were appointed scrutineers, and the ballot was a tie. It was decided, after a season of prayer, to cast lots for the final decision ; when it resulted in favor of removal, and thus a vexed question was satisfactorily settled.

Elder Topping and R. H. Burtch were added to the site committee.

CHAPTER V.

April 16 it was moved by Deacon Winter, seconded by R. W.
Sawtell:

"That Rev. James Cooper be invited to take the pastoral
charge of this church ; that the salary be one hundred pounds
per annum ; that a subscription list be circulated forthwith."

At the same meeting Mr. Winter was authorised to attend
Hatch's sale of lots ; but not bid more than eight and one half
dollars per foot, for a suitable site for the church.

Peter and Duncan Campbell were received for baptism, and
William Nasmyth and Mrs. Morley by letter ; Arthur Miller
and George Duncan by baptism, and others during the summer
of 1854 ; and at the November meeting Deacon Winter and
wife, R. W. Sawtell and wife, received letters to unite with the
Brantford Church.

A reference might be permitted here, in regard to establishing a denominational paper : For a long time there had not
been a medium of communication by a paper of its own. "The
Observer" and others had ceased to exist.   Mr. Winter had laid
the matter to heart, and some time previously pledged himself
privately, " that the first sum of considerable importance which
came to him in any business transaction he would devote to
starting a denominational paper."

After settling in East Zorra two years before, he thought he
would have an interest in Woodstock, and purchased a lot from
Deacon Burtch for $300 (and subsequently many others, at

boom prices, caused by the Crimean war, and the building of the C. W R.) and, not long after, the Woodstock and Lake Erie R. R. Co. gave him about $4,000 for the same ; thus his request was granted, and he immediately proceeded to carry out his vow. The result was the establishment of "The Christian Messenger" in Brantford—with Rev. T. L. Davidson as editor and R. W. Sawtell sub-editor and office manager, the first copy of which was printed the 1st of October, 1854.

"The Messenger" was subsequently sold to Dr. Fyfe, renamed "The Canadian Baptist," and is still the organ of the denomination. As this paper has wielded such an influence, and particularly in the educational policy with which this church, through the location of the college here, has been so interested, this digression will not be deemed out of place.

November 25th, 1854, Deacon Blake resigned the trusteeship and Elder Topping was appointed in his place.

January 5th, 1855, "The Home Missionary Society of Canada" is first mentioned, and it was decided to take up a collection in its favor.

George Duncan preached his first sermon before the church and was granted a license to preach. He soon became well known as such, and was called to the pastorate of the Hamilton Church ; but died soon thereafter, quite young, and greatly lamented.

May 26th it was decided, by the casting vote of the pastor, not to make application for admission into the association, or send delegates thereto. At the following meeting in June, it was moved by W. H. Landon, seconded by Deacon A. Burtch, and resolved, That the following clause be inserted in the church deed : "Holding and teaching the doctrines generally held by evangelical churches, and also the baptism of adult believers, in the name of the Holy Trinity, as the only Christian baptism in water, and the administration of the ordinance of the Lord's Supper to persons who have been so baptised only."

September 29th the higher education question is first introduced, and a resolution passed authorising Messrs. Cooper, Topping, Burtch and Martin "to examine the constition of

Maclay College, and point out those articles necessary to be amended."

November 24th the following resolutions were passed:

1. "That Elder Cooper's travelling expenses to St. Catharines, to attend the missionary meeting held there the last of the month, be paid."

2. "That the new chapel be opened at Christmas and Sabbath previous."

Several committees were appointed for various purposes in connection with said dedication.

December 29, 1855, another long list of resolutions were passed: "That the seats be rented."

(2). "That door keepers show strangers to any vacant seats after the unlet ones are filled."

(3). "That the price of the pews be £5, £4, £3 and £2 and the price of a single sitting one-fourth the price of a whole seat."

(4). "The committee to take charge of this work."

(5). "That the trustees be empowered to insure the chapel for £1,500."

(6). "That the report of the finances of the building committee be laid before next church meeting."

(7). "That George Duncan have a letter of dismission."

(8). "That Elders Cooper, Landon and Topping attend the council at Hamilton to ordain Bro. Duncan."

The minutes furnish no description of the new building but very many remember it as it stood where the present church now stands, and a lithograph of which hangs in many of the older members' houses with the difference that the spire was never completed. The building was of Gothic design, and considered very beautiful in appearance; but, like many other buildings of that day, it was placed too low in the ground, making the basement too damp and dark for Sunday school and other purposes.

There was a great deal of trouble about the site, there being some shadow upon the title, and another site was purchased on

Bay street and had to be disposed of after finally decidirg on the present one, corner of Beale and Adelaide streets. There are several resolutions, subsequently, instructing the trustees to complete the spire but it was never done, it being held that the tower was not equal to the strain that would be put upon it.

The old chapel and site were sold to Mr. Mills and a resolution passed February 4th, 1856, confirming the sale and providing for removing the dead buried on the lot. The chapel was subsequently moved to the grounds of old St. Paul's church and used for a school room till a few years ago when it was destroyed by fire. At the same meeting the trustees were instructed to sell the Bay street lot for not less than £300.

May 31st a constitution was adopted governing the proceedings of the "Woodstock Baptist Missionary Society."

Rev. J. Cooper, Rev. W. H. Landon, A. Miller, J. Hatch and J. Martin were appointed delegates to the Grand River Association, to be held at Brantford June 13th, with instructions as follows: "That this church reserve to itself as an independent church of Christ the privilege of discipling its own members, settling its own ministers and regulating its own terms of communion as now practiced among us, notwithstanding any previous acts or resolves of said association.

At the following church meeting, June 4th, the draft of the letter to the association being read, it was resolved "That the instructions passed by resolution at the last meeting be expunged and that the delegates leave the question in abeyance, unless the association introduce it." The statistics were: received by letter 15, by baptism 15, dismissed 1, died 1, total in good standing 109.

June 28, 1856, the following resolutions were passed, viz.:

1. "That Mr. Cooper's salary be raised £25 for the present year."

2. "That John Midgley receive a recommendation to exercise his talent wherever he may be called."

3. "That the said John Midgley have his seat free."

4. "That the following report of the delegates to the G. R. Association be adopted."

The report is too long to be repeated here, but the purport is: That the delegates were questioned very closely on the subject of communion and the practice of the church ; and in their answers the delegates disagreed. A. Miller claimed " the privilege of communing when and with whom he might choose." This led to a very sharp discussion and the result was that the church was not admitted into the association ; but it was recommended that the application be laid over till the next association, and that the church be respectfully requested to call a council to discuss the whole question, and formally recognize it, in the meantime.

5. " That this church does not approve of its members communing with churches of other denominations."

6. " That Bro. Miller's confession be accepted as satisfactory."

The first reference to the "Baptist Academy" being likely to be located here, appears in the minutes of the church meeting held February 28, 1857, when it was resolved, "That we, as a Close Communion Baptist church, consider ourselves as part and parcel of, and in communion with, the Regular Baptists of this Province."

At the same meeting it was decided to discontinue the seat renting system, and adopt the voluntary subscription plan—but to allot the seats to subscribers.

April 25 it was resolved, " That we have always, as a church, considered it unscriptural for any member to administer the ordinance of Baptism, or the Lord's Supper, except those who have been ordained to the work of the ministry ; and anyone doing so is liable to church discipline."

May 10th, 1857, after the morning service the members were requested to remain, to consider the question of calling a council of recognition. Mr. Topping reported that the committee appointed to solicit subscriptions to the fund for the erection of the Literary Institute, "found it difficult to prevail, on account of the position of the Woodstock Church, it being unconnected with the association as a Regular Baptist Church. He therefore moved, seconded by Deacon Burtch, " That a council be called. It was moved in amendment by Elder Landon, seconded by A. Miller, "That a meeting be held on the following Tuesday to decide the matter." The amendment carried.

The meeting was held, as per adjournment, when it was unanimously decided to call a council, and the following were appointed delegates, viz.: Revs. J. Cooper, E. Topping, and Deacons Burtch and Hatch.

If a council of recognition was convened here there is no minute of such.

May 30, 1837, it was resolved, "That this church make application to the "Grand River Association South" for admission, and that Messrs. Cooper, Topping, Burtch, Hatch and Sawtell be our delegates to the same."

June 26, 1857 The delegates to the association, which was held at Harris street, reported that "this church was cordially and unanimously admitted into the association."

At this meeting a resolution was passed condemning the action of one of our unordained members, he having administered the ordinance of baptism, and warned not to do so again.

Sept 6th. The church discussed the question of singing; after which "Mrs. Landon was appointed to take the lead of the female department," and "R. H. Burtch and W. Nasmyth the male department, with power to add to their number." This is the first official appointment of this nature referred to.

Another reference of still greater importance to this church, and to the whole denomination, is this: "That as Mr. Fyfe, of Toronto, has leave of absence, and as he has consented to stay throughout the week, be it therefore—"Resolved that a series of meetings be held in the basement every evening, at half-past seven o'clock, and that brethren sustain such meetings by their presence and prayers."

From this time forward the question of Baptist ministerial education became so closely connected with this church, that the origin of the movement should find a place here. The denomination had established Montreal college, and, for want of funds, and a general sympathy in its management, it had died. A

C

project had also been started to establish what was to be called Maclay college, and that never found even a commencement.

The establishment of "The Christian Messenger" gave opportunity for the expression of matters of denominational interest, and the question of education was one of the most prominent, and frequently referred to. In "The Messenger" of December 13th, 1855, a "Proposal," over the signature of "F"—written, no doubt, by Dr. Fyfe—and from which the project of an academy, such as the Woodstock school became, was advocated. The agitation was continued, through that medium and otherwise, until it was finally adopted.

It was decided by the preliminary committee that the location should not be cast of St. Catharines or west of London, and the place which made the best offer in regard to the erection of buildings should be chosen. The only places which tendered were: Fonthill, Brantford and Woodstock. The latter offered more than twice as much as Brantford, guaranteeing $16,000, including the value of the site, and Woodstock was chosen.

The first meeting of subscribers was held in the church on the 18th of March, 1857. William Winter was elected chairman, and R. W. Sawtell, secretary.

A constitution and by-law previously prepared were discussed and adopted. The following were the first trustees, viz: A. Burtch, E. Topping, J. Hatch, A. Carroll, J. Kintrea, J. Charles, W. Winter, T. L. Davidson, R. A. Fyfe, H. J. Barber, W. Wilkinson, O. Mabee, R. Kilborn, R. Baker, E. V. Bodwell.

W. Winter was elected president, J. Hatch vice-president, James Kintrea treasurer, and E. V. Bodwell secretary.

On the 23rd of June the corner stone of the first building was laid. Deacon Burtch had the honor of that duty. Addresses were made by W. Winter, Revs. R. A. Fyfe, T. L. Davidson and W. Wilkinson. E. V. Bodwell, George Alexander and Rev. Dr. Ryerson, chief superintendent of education. Thus the foundation of an enterprise was then laid which has had a direct influence on this church and a mighty power in molding and building up the denomination throughout the province, as

well as establishing and carrying on the grand missionary work
in India and the Home Mission work in Canada.

The pew rent system was still unsettled, for we find that at
the church meeting held 27th of November a resolution appointing R. W. Sawtell, F. Scofield and Peter Campbell, a committee
"to appraise and regulate the seat rents, and report at our
anniversary,"

"That we have anniversary services. That Pastor Cooper and
E. Topping be a committee to invite speakers, and the ladies
have the sole power to arrange the festival and appoint their
own committees." No further mention of the "festival" is
made ; but it took place, was well attended and successful.

On the 27th of December Elder Cooper's heart was made
glad by the acceptance of his son, George, as a fit candidate for
baptism. Morris Dawes was also received.

January 3rd, 1858, Deacon Burtch and Brother Shanks were
appointed to visit members absenting themselves from the
communion and other services.

The same question of delinquency was still before the church;
but it is noticed that it is shifted from " the covenant meeting"
to the ".communion service "—showing that the meetings, for
so many years considered the all-important, now became only
secondary. At this same meeting the question of "alteration
in our church meetings and ordinance day was up for discussion
and postponed to next regular meeting."

Messrs. Laycock, Nasmyth, Carryer and Luck were appointed
a committee "to devise means to refund money advanced by the
treasurer."

On the 30th of January it was resolved, "That the monthly
church meetings be held on the Friday previous to the first
Sabbath of every month, at 2.30 p. m., and that all pecuniary
matters be taken up at the close of the religious exercises";
"That a donation visit be made to Mr. Cooper, at his own
house, on Monday, the 8th of February."

CHAPTER VI.

FINANCIAL PRESSURE—FINANCE COMMITTEE APPOINTED—ELECTION
OF DEACONS—THE CHAPEL ON FIRE—QUESTION OF PRIVILEGE—
OPENING OF THE C. L. I , DR. FYFE PRINCIPAL—PRINCE OF
WALES' VISIT—BURNING OF THE INSTITUTE.

The question of finances was a pressing one at this period.
The collapse after the Crimean war was severely felt, and as a
consequence church finances suffered also. At the March meeting the Finance committee reported as follows: "From ladies
association $50, building fund $16, pastor's subscripton $8, in-
cidental $2, and as nothing farther at present can be collected
from the building list that a number of the members sign a note
for £50 to relieve present needs," &c. The report which is long
and relates to the difficulties under which they had labored, and
suggesting that it was the duty of every one to do all they could,
was adopted.

Brother and Sister Pavey requested letters of dismission to
join the Free Will Baptist church organized in their neighbor-
hood, which was granted under the circumstances referred to.

April 2nd, 1858, a committee reported on the continued
absence and removal of a number of members and recommended
dropping their names from the church roll. Report adopted.

W. Nasmyth, H. T. Burtch and D. Campbell were appointed
to assist the deacons collect for church funds.

W. Nasmyth appointed financial secretary in the room of C.
C. Carryer, resigned.

April 30th, Rev. George Silver, wife and mother, were received
by letter from the Peekskill Baptist church, United States, and
a number of candidates for baptism.

The trustees were authorized to borrow from the Trust and
Loan Company, by mortgage on the church property.

June 4th, Elders Cooper and Topping, brethren A. Burtch, J. Hatch, R H. Burtch and J. Peddie were elected delegates to the Grand River Association South.

July 2nd, the same delegates were appointed to sit in council with the church in Ingersoll which sat last spring, viz: Revs. J. Cooper, E. Topping and Deacon Burtch, with Rev. G. Silver added.

"That Mrs. Burtch, Silver, Lamport and Hatch be a committee of ladies to collect subscription to make up the deficit in in the pastor's salary.

"That D. Campbell circulate a list to raise money to pay for attending and cleaning the chapel.

This was the continual experience, little money moving and a severe trial to get enough to pay current expenses. Not a meeting passing free from financial embarrassments.

November 5th, it was resolved "That those absent members written to and who have not answered be dropped from our books as members."

"That R. H. Burtch, H. T. Burtch and S. Pocock be a committee to erect a shed--if it can be accomplished with little or no expense."

"That the church meetings be changed from Friday afternoon to Saturday afternoon for religious exercises only, and special meetings for business called when needed."

January 13th, 1859, it was resolved (1) "That Elder Cooper and Bro. Midgley be our delegates to the Nissouri council to organize a church in the Vining settlement."

(2) "That Brethren Topping, Nasmyth, Lamport and Martin be appointed to draw out a report of the best mode of liquidating our debts."

(3). "That Brethren Nasmyth and Sawtell be committee to arrange for better church music, with power to add to their number."

Messrs. Topping, Blake and Hatch were appointed to collect for the missionary convention.

The church seems to have been passing through financial

troubles at this time. All manner of means and modes were adopted to collect funds, but no one seems to have been able. Mr. Cooper's little salary was in arrears to the amount of $340, and he was taking all kinds of produce in pay. It was only by the utmost economy that he was enabled to maintain his family and give them an education.

The hardness of the times gave rise to the appointment of a financial committee. We find that on February 17th, 1859, the auditors report was received and adopted ; that the report of the financial committee be adopted and, brethren Hatch, Topping, Lamport and J. Muir appointed to carry out its suggestions. "That a social tea meeting be held in the basement on the evening of the second Thursday in March. and a free-will offering be taken to assist in paying off the $260 arrears due the pastor. That Mrs. Burtch and Mrs. Lamport be a committee to make arrangements for said social."

Monday evening, February 21st, an adjourned church meeting was held for the purpose of discussing the question of election of deacons and deciding the method. It was finally agreed that the pastor preach a special sermon referring to the qualifications required in the office of Deacon. After the service open nominations be made, and two weeks thereafter elected by ballot."

On Sabbath, March 6th, after communion the following were nominated: H. Lamport, F. Scofield, T. Clifford, E. Topping, C. C. Carryer, R. W. Sawtell, G. Luck.

R. W. Sawtell was appointed secretary of the social committee, and a committee of four brethren "to receive and value the gifts."

An opportunity was given to those who did not wish to serve as deacon if elected to decline, when R. W. Sawtell, F. Schofield and G. Luck asked to be allowed to retire, which was granted.

On March 20th the meeting was held to decide by ballot the choice for deacons, when it was resolved "That as Bro. Topping had already been a Deacon of his church and ordained thereto that he be recognised by a vote of this church as one of its Deacons.—Carried. C. C. Carryer and T. Cliffoad refused to be

FIRST BAPTIST CHURCH.

 39

balloted for and only H. Lamport was left and he was declared elected.

April 13th the trustees were instructed to reconvey the Bay-st. lot back to the Hatch estate, if requested and found necessary.

May 15th Messrs. Cooper, Burtch, Topping, Sawtell and Midgley were appointed delegates to the association.

A resolution was passed requesting W. M. Mills to delay removing the dead from the old grave yard, till the trustees had notified all the friends of such removal.

W. Nasmyth's resignation as leader of the singing was accepted, and R. H. Burtch, J. Martin and the pastor appointed to arrange for a leader.

July 14th E. Topping and A. Burtch were appointed a committee to visit the Burford and Blenheim friends and collect funds for the pastor's salary. That the discussion on the pastor's salary be adjourned to a special meeting, when all the friends of the congregation shall be invited to attend. That Pastor Cooper and Elder Topping visit several members who have long absented themselves from communion and fellowship of the church.

A special meeting was held July 21st when, on motion of W. J. Copp, one large committee was appointed for the town, and a smaller one for the county, to canvass for subscriptions, "to be paid quarterly, to make up deficiencies in the pastor's salary."

Delegates were appointed, September 8th, to attend a council at Springford, to ordain Mr. Mudge to the work of the ministry.

It appears from the record that a number, whose names are given, had absented themselves from church privileges for some time, and at this meeting asked for letters of dismission on the ground that some of the members "were destitute of Christian character"; and without making specific charges. After fully discussing the matter it was

Resolved, "That it would be inconsistent with church order to grant letters under such circumstances. If the charges were true, our letters would be valueless; and if untrue, they greatly err in asking letters on a false foundation. Meantime we drop their names from the church roll."

November 10th, 1859, a committee, which had for a long
period been negotiating a settlement with Mr. Mills in regard
to the old burying ground, reported at this meeting that no arrangement could be come to, hence they would recommend that
they advertise in The Sentinel, notifying all parties having dead
buried therein to remove the same by the 1st of December, and
that Deacons Burtch and Lamport be a committee to assist such
parties."

Sabbath day, January 1st, 1860, application was made by
Brother and Sister Favey, by letter, to unite with this church ;
also their daughter Belinda, all from East Zorra Church.

On the following Sabbath, January 8th, this record appears :
" In the time of worship our chapel took fire, and after consid-
erable exertion by all the people, the flames were extinguished.
The following committee was then and there appointed to see
the damages repaired, viz : Deacon Hatch, E. Topping, W. J.
Copp, H. T. Burtch and Deacon Burtch.

The fire originated in the floor, from overheating, it being a
very cold day ; and was extinguished largely with snow, carried
in by those present, and the damages were not extensive.

February 14th a special meeting was held for the purpose of
discussing a question of privilege. It appears that one of the
deacons (Lamport) had, in his zeal, invited Elder George Wilson,
then a noted evangelist, to come and carry on special services.
He, having accepted the invitation, took full possession of the
work and so thoroughly ignored the pastor, and introduced
methods which Mr. Cooper and many of the brethren could not
endorse ; hence this meeting was called to correct the error.

E. Topping was appointed chairman, and R. W. Sawtell secretary.

Mr. Cooper was called upon for a statement of the case ; after
which Deacon Lamport said that if he had done wrong he was
sorry for it, as he intended neither wrong or insult to anyone.

Elder Wilson, being present, explained his position, and was
fully exonerated from blame.

On Motion of R. W. Sawtell, seconded by Bro. Carryer, the

following resolution was passed : " That this church discounte nances and condemns any effort of, or influence used, by any member or members to introduce any minister or layman with a view to assist or supercede the efforts of the pastor of this church, for the time being, without the concurrence of the pastor and church."

A vote of sympathy with the pastor, and entire confidence in his labors, was passed and tendered to Elder Cooper.

April 5th many old troubles were brought up and discussed: 1. In reference to settling with Mr. Mills about the grave yard. 2. Refusing letters of dismission to embarrassed debtors. 3. Financial shortage. 4. Appointing a committee to classify, and present at next meeting a list of non-members. 6. That any member absenting himself or herself from communion on three consecutive Sabbaths, be visited and be liable to church discipline, if without valid excuse.

It is evident from the minutes of the meetings held in this particular period of the church's history that the question of close communion was bearing heavily on many of the formerly active members. While very few practised communing with Pedo-Baptist churches, they could not brook the dictation and withdrew, largely, from active work in the church. Many names were dropped, and some few were excluded ; thus to ensure the fullest concurrence to the practice of a " Regular Baptist Church." Many of such have since returned and became both active and consistent members.

May 24th, 1860, the pastor, E. Topping, and J. Martin were appointed to write the circular letter, Messrs. Cooper,Topping. Burtch, Lamport and George Cooper were appointed delegates to the association, with power to invite it to meet here in 1861.

This was an eventful year to the Baptists of Ontario and especially to the Woodstock church. Since the meeting held on the 18th of March, 1857, the Canadian Literary Institute had. been erected, and, by toils and sacrifices---which would require a volume to relate---the building had been equipped, and made ready for opening, Dr. Fyfe chosen principal, with Rev. W.

Stewart, Mr. Hankinson, Miss Brigham and Miss Vining, teachers. This was a small staff and the salaries promised were equally small; but they entered upon the work with loving hearts and active brains. The coming to this town of a band of teachers and an indefinite number of students, many of whom had and would devote their talents to God's service, meant new ideas and new work for the church.

One of the first things Dr. Fyfe was called upon to do was to read an address, from the trustees of the Institute, to the Prince of Wales, who was then making a tour on this continent, and who was entertained on Cottle's Grove. Many addresses were read; and probably the most attractive was the one read by Mr. Fyfe. He was then one of the handsomest of men, and called forth the remark from the Prince : that "he was the finest specimen of man he had met."

The school opened in July, had two sessions that fall, and closed in December with increasing prospects for the new year— 1861 ; but, on the night preceding its opening, the whole structure was laid in ruins by fire. It is not the intention of this sketch to embrace that of the college also, but the interests of the church have been so involved with the college that we cannot ignore some of its more important events, and this is one of them.

The blotting out of the school would naturally withdraw life, numbers and activity from the church ; but its rebuilding would mean additional financial burdens. The latter prevailed, but was cheerfully accepted, and resulted in greater prosperity, both in educational work and church extension. Thus an apparently disastrous fire, in the providence of God, united the denomination in sympathy and support in the cause of higher and ministerial education.

CHAPTER VII.

Stringent Times Still—Trouble Satisfactorily Settled—Elder Cooper's Resignation Not Acceptable—Subsequently Accepted—Dr. Fyfe and Rev. W.Stewart Supply the Pulpit—Call to Rev. W. H. Jones—Installation Services.

All through the year 1860 various means were suggested and some schemes adopted to pay pressing debts. In November Mr. Cooper's salary was raised " to the original $500." R. H. Burtch resigned the leadership of the choir, and Mr. Zimmerman was appointed in his place. Mr. Topping resigned his position as trustee, and Brother Pavey was appointed in his place.

In December W. B. Hankinson, W. J. Copp, R. Cull and wife and others were baptized, and some received by letter. A successful anniversary was held, the proceeds of which were used to pay interest on the church site.

Thus the old year ended and the new year began, and now were added the additional burdens of the Institute. On the 1st day of January a special meeting was held to devise ways and means ; and one of the resolutions adopted was a twenty-five-cent plan for the debts of the Institute, and a committee of ladies to carry it out.

J. R. Cook and wife were received by letter from St. Catharines. James Martin resigned as clerk, treasurer and deacon, and E. Topping was appointed clerk pro tem ; C. C. Carryer, treasurer.

The committee appointed to raise money to pay off the debt upon the chapel reported that they only required one hundred and twenty five dollars more to complete the amount and a special effort was to be made to finish the whole sum. At a subsequent meeting in March it is reported that the full amount had been subscribed.

At the April meeting James Cox was appointed church clerk and C. C. Carryer, treasurer.

The 28th of May the committee appointed to visit Mr. Luck reported that he had joined the Plymouth brethren, whereupon it was resolved "that the hand of fellowship be withdrawn from him for dereliction of duty and non attendance."

The Pastor, Deacons Burtch and Hatch and brethren Topping and Pavey, were appointed delegates to the association to be held in the Woodstock church.

Messrs. Topping and Clifford were appointed to sit in council to recognize the Wellesly church.

June 28th, Jno. R. Cook and W. Pavey were appointed deacons.

It is but right to refer here to a matter that had occupied the attention of the church for many months. Miss Crosbie had come to Woodstock under expectation of being appointed lady principal of the Institute, but was not elected to that position. She had been permitted to commune with the church but in her disappointment in failing to be appointed had said some unjust things about the pastor. Mr. Cooper asked for an investigation which was held and fully exonerated him. Mr. Martin, who had in the meantime married Miss Crosbie, defended her case, and took such a violent part against the pastor and officers of the church that after every attempt to reconcile him was made without avail: it was moved by Bro. Topping, seconded by Bro. Evans, and resolved "That the church regrets that Bro. Martin persists in his groundless charges against the pastor, and that in accepting his resignation, they are, by his own action, shut up to the necessity of withdrawing from him the hand of fellowship).

November 14th, the Pastor and E. Topping were appointed delegates to attend at the Horton street church, London, to ordain Benjamin Miller, and the expenses of said delegates to be paid by this church unless paid by the London church.

At the first communion Sabbath in January, 1862, Mr. and Mrs. Fyfe asked permission to commune with the church for a time without uniting.

At the same time Elder Cooper stated that he had heard of some dissatisfaction in regard to himself, and he wished to state that he was prepared to resign if the church thought it best.

January 16th, the committee appointed to raise money to pay arrears of the pastor's salary, gave a very discouraging report and asked for another month's time.

It was also decided to hold a social to assist the committee in their efforts—the arrears due the pastor November 1st last being $241.50. It was also decided to hold a special meeting to discuss the proposed resignation of the Pastor.

John R. Cook was appointed leader of the choir. H. Burtch having intimated that he did not consider himself the leader and "if the parties composing said choir do not conduct themselves in a becoming manner after being spoken to that Bro. Cook expel them from the choir under sanction of this church."

Special meeting held 30th January, to consider Mr. Cooper's resignation.

Moved by R. W. Sawtell, seconded by W. J. Copp, "that the church do not consider that the resignation of the pastor would advance the cause in this place or be of any advantage to the church, neither is it now required of him ; and further the church would regret to learn of any serious disaffection felt by any members of the church toward him, either as a brother or pastor. And we take this opportunity to express our entire confidence in him as a pastor and esteem as a brother."

On a division being taken after much discussion there were 50 for and 11 against the resolution.

It was resolved "That the students of the Institute who are members of Regular Baptist churches be admitted to a seat with us at communion on bringing letters of recommendation from such churches."

At the church meeting held March 18 it was resolved, " That Elder Cooper's resignation be accepted. That a pulpit supply committee be appointed. That all be requested to make quarterly payments of pew rent, in advance, to enable the treasurer to settle with the retiring pastor. That R. H. Burtch and J. R. Cook audit the treasurer's books."

April 10th Deacons Lamport and Cook tendered their resignation of the office of deacon—laid over one month.

Elders Cooper, Stewart and Deacon Burtch were appointed a committee to confer with the colored brethren, in reference to the formation of a church for themselves, and report at next meeting.

April 24th the resignation of Deacon Lamport was accepted.

The committee reported in favor of the colored people forming a church, if they felt desirous. The sexton's salary (Mr. Godfrey) was advanced to $24 per annum. Letters of dismission were granted to Mr. and Mrs. Cooper and George Cooper.

Delegates were asked to sit in council in the Sprague settlement, to recognize a church there. E. Topping, J. R. Cook and George Blake were appointed. R. A. Fyfe and wife presented their letters from the Toronto Bond Street Church, and received the hand of fellowship on Sabbath, September 7th. On the 25th of the same month Dr. Fyfe proposed to the church, that if they would raise a special contribution to pay off a debt of $800, then due on the church site, he and Rev. W. Stewart would supply the pulpit one year free.

This generous offer was gratefully accepted, and a committee appointed to carry it out.

At the church meeting in November it was decided to hold a public meeting on "Thanksgiving day"—the first of the kind mentioned. It was held accordingly and well attended. After it terminated it was resolved, "That the church co-operate with the "ladies sewing socciety" in holding a teameeting to clear off the debt on the chapel"—the ladies to name the day. No further mention is made regarding the teameeting.

During the year 1862 many members were added by Baptism. On Sabbath, January 25th, a resolution was passed inviting Rev. Mr. Winterbotham to come to assist for two or three weeks. Later on Elder Geary was invited and came, who, with the assistance of Elder Topping and others, held evening meetings. Brethren Nasmyth, Copp and Cox were appointed to make provision for the Sabbath day singing.

A revising of the church roll took place, and many names were dropped at a special meeting in February. A report from the committee stated, "that with all their efforts they were $200 short of the $800 required." Eight persons, then present, guaranteed the payment of the required amount, with the understanding that the church should make an effort to assist them.

May 21st letters of dismission were given to the Gobles, Kipps and others. Elders Fyfe and Topping and Brethren Pavey, Cook and Burtch were appointed delegates to the association, to be held at Springford ; Rev. W. Stewart and the clerk to prepare the letter.

Dr. Fyfe requested leave from pastoral duties for six weeks' vacation. Rev. W. Stewart asked to be relieved from his last three Sabbath's supply, on account of his leaving for Brantford. Both requests were granted. That Deacon Burtch and W. Nasmyth be the supply committee. That the church buy six music books for the use of the choir.

At the July meeting the thanks of the church were tendered, publicly, to Bro. W. Stewart, for his gratuitous and efficient services in the pulpit ; and letters of dismission to the Brantford Church, for himself and wife, were granted.

September 28th Brethren Copp, Pavey, Burtch and Topping were appointed a committee to co-operate with the English Church people in the purchase of a piece of land for a cemetery. "That the committee use $225 of the site funds (not yet required) to purchase said site, and close the transaction at once."

A special meeting was held October 14th for the purpose of discussing the calling of a pastor. Rev. S. W. Walden, of Dunkirk, was mentioned, and Elder Topping appointed to make enquiries.

On the 3rd of November Mr. Topping read a letter in reference to the call, which was not considered favorable. Rev. Thos. Henderson was then invited to fill the pulpit three or four weeks.

A resolution, conveying the cordial thanks of the church to Dr. Fyfe, for his efficient services for the year, was passed. That Brother Carryer's resignation as treasurer be not accepted till the end of the year. That a teameeting be held on Christmas Day ; the proceeds to be applied towards the $800 debt on the site.

Dr. Fyfe was appointed a delegate to the ordination of Bro. F. Ratcliffe.

Church meeting, December 17th, resolutions passed : "That Deacons Pavey, Burtch and Nasmyth be a supply committee. That the treasurer exchange the silver on hand at the best advantage, and lodge the same in the savings bank. That W. Nasmyth be the treasurer from and after the 1st of January, 1864. That the deacons assume and take charge of the sacrament funds. That a committee of ladies be appointed to collect Home Mission funds. That the pew rents be raised to meet the pastor's salary."

Special meeting, January 25, 1864 : " That we give the Rev. W. H. Jones, of Port Hope, a call to become the pastor ; that we offer him six hundred dollars per annum, payable in advance quarterly. That Brother Willis be appointed usher. That Dr. Fyfe be requested to speak to the students about seating and collections."

February 18th a letter was read from Rev. W. H. Jones, accepting the call to him, to commence the first Sabbath in May.

After service, Sabbath, May 1st, the following resolution was passed : " That we have installation services on the 11th of May, and that the pastor (W. H. Jones), Brethren Cox, Topping and Cook be a committee to make the necessary arrangements ; and the expenses of ministers attending from a distance, be paid.

May 19th the clerk and Elder Topping were appointed to write the circular letter, and the pastor, Brethren Brett, Topping, R. H. Burtch, Nasmyth and Willis be the delegates to the association.

J. E. Wells and wife were received by letter from Albert's County, New Brunswick..

At the special meeting June 8th the deacons recommended the appointment of a finance committee " to carry out a better plan of raising money for the various objects ; to print and circulate cards showing the needed objects, and have parties subscribe." This was, in part, the initiation of the present method, but not fully carried out.

Special meeting, 22nd June, James Martin asked to be restored to membership—granted. " That the motion for the calling of stated monthly church meetings be rescinded, and be called hereafter by the pastor. That a social be held on Thursday, 30th instant, the proceeds to be devoted to renovating the pulpit and providing a new Bible and hymn book. That we present those now used to the colored brethren for use in their chapel." W. J. Copp and wife and W. Burtch received letters of dismission.

July 27 the pastor, Dr. Fyfe, Deacons Pavey and Cook were delegated to attend the ordination of R. B. Montgomery, to be held at the Scotland Church.

August 17th the former negotiations for a site for a cemetery having failed, a committee was appointed " to find another site, with the same powers as the former committee. That the forty dollars expenses, incurred by the pastor for removal from Port Hope, be paid."

November 16th E. Topping was elected trustee in place of Mr. Landon, who had removed from town.

Deacon Pavey reported, on the 26th January, 1865, that there was "a want of harmony " in the Board of Deacons and that, consequently, he would resign. A committee was appointed to enquire into the matter, and the result was that a new election of deacons took place. Dr. Fyfe preached a sermon, setting forth the duties and privileges of the office ; after which W. Pavey, J. Cox, T. G. Clifford and R. Cull were elected deacons. A. Burtch was appointed an honorary deacon.

April 4th A. E. Willis was appointed sexton at the rate of $1 per week. The trustees were asked to attend to the repairs of the church, and also the ventilation of the same.

D

June 14th Bro. J. L. Campbell was granted a license to exercise his gifts and to enable him to enter as a theological student, and to receive ministerial aid.

September 8th the pastor and Brethren Topping, Clark and Midgley were appointed to sit in council at Embro, for the purpose of organizing a church there.

A committee was appointed to investigate the title of the site, and the terms of the mortgage thereon, and settle the same.

CHAPTER VIII.

DEATH OF DEACON BURTCH—BURNING OF THE CHAPEL—RESIGNATION
OF PASTOR JONES—WITHDRAWAL FROM THE DENOMINATION—RE-
ERECTION OF THE CHURCH—OPENING OF THE BASEMENT - CALL TO
ELDER BATES—HIS ACCEPTANCE—BRO. TIMPANY—OUR FIRST
MISSIONARY—OPENING OF THE AUDIENCE ROOM—PROTEST AGAINST
THE USE OF THE ORGAN.

January 5th, 1866, dear old Deacon Burtch passed over to .the "Great Majority," and "the place that has known him so long, shall know him no more forever." It may be truly said: "this day a prince has fallen in Israel!" From the day of his "new birth" and entrance into this church—August 28th, 1824—to the day of his death (nearly 44 years), never had a church a more faithful member, or more zealous and watchful deacon—always at his post, always liberal in support and hospitable to all—strangers as well as friends. The latch string of his door was always out to every weary traveller or benighted, footsore pilgrim in the wilderness. The Canadian Literary Institute, as well as the church, may be said to owe its continued existence to his sacrificial love; for when in the deep waters of financial distress, he mortaged his own home to rescue it from bankruptcy.

What more need be said? An interesting volume might be written in commemoration of the life of this faithful servant of the Lord, and friend of humanity ; but this is not the time or place to do more than record these facts. His memory is enshrined in our hearts and " his works do follow him."

Sabbath morning, January 21, 1866 It is here recorded that "this morning between two and three o'clock, the wind blowing a hurricane, our chapel was burnt to the ground and nothing saved. Had preaching in the Institute in the morning; Sabbath School in the Free Baptist Church, afternoon ; and service in the town hall in the evening. Rev. Mr. Baldwin, of Ingersoll preached on behalf of the missionary convention. Rev. W. H. Jones preaching in Ingersoll at the same time." Such is the brief record of a disaster that the church could ill afford and which involved more work and greater sacrifice on the part of the members.

Immediate preparations were made for rebuilding. committees were appointed, subscription lists circulated and past liabilities pressed for payment. The pastor, believing that the church could not rebuild and maintain a pastor at the same time, tendered his resignation, which was accepted to terminate at the end of his year, 1st of May. He to have leave of absence to visit other places.

On the 22nd of February Dr. Fyfe reported " that the committee on sites had seen Mr. Cottle and were of the opinion that the old site should be given up and a new one selected, as there would not be time to settle the validity of the title in time to re build there this summer."

It appears that there was some defect in the title which had not been discovered till recently, and now the question of the liability of the trustees was to be referred to a chancery lawyer and Dr. Fyfe, E. Topping and W. Pavey were authorized to act in the interest of the church.

Messrs. Biggins, Nasmyth and Carryer were appointed to secure plans for a new building not to exceed in cost of building $5,000.

At an adjourned meeting, 12th of March, Dr. Fyfe reported that the committee had seen a chancery lawyer who assured them that the trustees were not responsible for the claim against the site. The church decided to tender the principal and 'all interest thereon, originally agreed to with Messrs. Deeds and De-Blaquier. J. E. Wells was granted a license to preach.

April 19th, James Cox resigned his offices of deacon and church clerk.

A letter from John Greig acting for Mr. Betteridge was read, agreeing to accept from the church the sum offered, viz : $1, 021,08 and guaranteeing a proper deed.

A pulpit supply committee was appointed with instruction "not to pay more than four dollars per Sabbath."

A building committee consisting of Messrs. Biggins, Cox, Sco-field, R. H. Burtch and W. Pavey was appointed.

Mr. Biggins plans were adopted and the committee instructed to advertise for tenders.

Rev. W. H. Jones publicly announced his intention to with-draw from the fellowship of this church and the denomination.

It was therefore resolved "That this church withdraws the hand of fellowship from him and records its disapproval of his concealing his change of views till the end of his pastorate."

Delegates to the association, Fyfe, Topping, Pavey, Midgley and Willis.

The use of the town hall to hold services therein during the rebuilding of the church was asked, and obtained.

The building committee were instructed to proceed with the re-erection on the same site.

September 30th, Dr. Fyfe, E. Topping and W. Pavey were appointed delegates to the Beachville church to sit in council.

The monthly church meetings were fixed on the third Wednes-day in each month after prayer meeting.

Oct. 14th, Dr. Fyfe and J. Cox were delegated to sit in coun-cil in Toronto to recognize the Alexander Street Church.

R. H. Burtch was appointed church clerk in place of John Midgley, resigned.

January 22nd, 1867, committees were appointed to arrange for a teameeting. Tickets 40cts. or two for 75cts.

The mechanics' hall was engaged for use, and a resolution passed to secure a pastor as early as possible.

March 28th, the trustees were requested "to purchase a piece of land for a cemetery and to confer with Deacon Pavey on the subject."

The basement of the new church was used for the first time March 31st, when Rev. W. Stewart, of Brantford, preached in the morning and Rev Jas. Cooper in the evening. Dr. Fyfe baptized several candidates in the afternoon.

The Sabbath school again took up its position, but in a largely improved room. It was larger, higher ceilings and better lighted and ventilated.

April 3rd, it was resolved "That we give the Rev. John Bates, now of Dundas, a call to the pastorate of the church."— Carried unanimously. "That six hundred dollars per annum be the salary paid."

A very cordial vote of thanks was passed to the Mayor and town council "for the use of the hall during the time of the rebuilding of the church."

May 7th, Dr. Fyfe was delegated to sit in council at Strathroy. Brother Galloway preached before the church and was granted a license to preach.

R. H. Burtch resigned as clerk and Deacon Carryer was appointed thereto.

Delegates were appointed to the association to be held at Mount Elgin, Dr. Fyfe to write the circular letter. Dr. Fyfe was delegated to sit in council with the Orford church to ordain James Coutts.

A letter from Rev. John Bates was read accepting the pastorate of the church to take place July 1st.

July 7th, Rev. John Bates entered upon his duties and baptized Mrs. Beard and Mary Pavey in the river Thames. Thus began a happy and prosperous pastorate.

A vote of thanks was tendered to W. Nasmyth for leading the singing for a long period. The committee to make arrangements for a new leader and proceed to collect funds for the purchase of an instrument "for the use of this chapel." That a tea meeting be held on the Tuesday following the Sabbath upon which the chapel is opened.

Several committees were appointed to make the necessary arrangements. These proceedings took place at the business meeting, Aug. 21st. On the first Sabbath in September Dr. Fyfe gave the right hand of fellowship to Pastor Bates, Mrs. S. Bates, Miss J. Bates, Miss M. Bates on their letters from the Dundas church.

October 7th, Revs. John Bates and R. A. Fyfe were appointed delegates to sit in council with the Brantford church to assist in the ordination of our dearly beloved brother Timpany, missionary elect for India.

The building committee made the announcement that the audience room would be ready for dedication by the 12th, and that date was then fixed for the purpose indicated.

The eventful day (October 13th, 1867) was duly honored, first by a special prayer meeting held in the basement at 10 a. m. At 11 a. m. Rev. Dr. Fyfe preached the dedicatory sermon to a very full house. Rev. T. L. Davidson, M. A., preached at 2.30 p. m., and the pastor, Rev. John Bates, at 6.30 p. m. The building was crowded to excess at each service. The collections amounted to eighty-eight dollars.

On Tuesday evening a tea meeting was held in the lecture room and the sum of $156.50 realized.

A platform meeting was held in the audience room when addresses of great interest were delivered and subscriptions taken equal to the remaining debt upon the building.

A vote of thanks was publicly tendered to Bro. W. Biggins for his fidelity and skill as the architect and superintendent of the building, thus saving—by adopting the system of day work instead of contracting—a large sum in its costs and also an assurance of better work.

October 24th, the caretaker's salary (Mr. Dawes) was increased to $2 per week. It was decided to upholster the seats with crimson damask. It was also resolved "That the church do promise to pay to the singing committee the sum of $50 for one year to aid them in procuring an organist." That we vote to Mr. Draper the sum of $10 for his services as leader."

December 18th, the following petition was presented: "That with heartfelt sorrow and love of the truth, we, the undersigned are under the necessity of entering our solemn protest against the use of instrumental music to praise God in the Sabbath services of the church, and consider the same an unscriptural innovation, calculated to destroy the pure, spiritual worship of the blessed Lord." (Sgd.) John Muir, James Martin, W. Duncan, Elizabeth Muir and Mary Whitehead.

The following resolution was passed in reply to the petitioners: "That while we respect these friends we do not see the matter as they do and to show that we wish to meet their wishes as far as we can we are willing to enter upon our church minutes their protest ; of course guarding ourselves from any endorsation of its sentiments."

This church has shared, to some extent, the old and deeply rooted prejudice against instrumental music. The first instance of trouble, in this respect, occurred in or about the year 1850. The singing was led at that time by an old settler by the name of James Merchant, assisted by R. H. and H. T. Burtch and R. W. Sawtell. Mr. Merchant could not always strike the key and he induced R. W. Sawtell to bring his flute and thus make sure. Occasionally the tune was new and difficult and he was asked to lead with the flute right through which he did, to the satisfaction of very many, but a few so strongly objected to "whistling God's praise through an instrument," that the flute was silenced and a tuning fork was substituted.

February 19th, 1868, a resolution was passed conferring power to the deacons to arrange and regulate the holding of all special meetings of the church. The Y. M. C. A. were granted the privilege of holding meetings in the church once in every two or three months.

Bro. J. J. Baker preached before the church at the Wednesday evening prayer meeting and on the 25th of March was "granted a license to preach, good for 12 months from date."

May 20th, 1868, Pastor Bates and Dr. Fyfe were appointed delegates to sit in council at Goble's corners with the view of recognizing a Baptist church there.

Brethren Topping, Hatch, Clifford, Willis, Carryer, Bates and Fyfe were appointed delegates to the association, to be held this year at Scotland, Bro. Bates to write the circular letter.

It will be remembered that at the platform meeting on the opening of the new audience room, it was announced that the debt was provided for.

At the special church meeting, July 22nd, the following resolutions was passed: "That the deacons and treasurer be requested to ascertain our indebtedness and to suggest some ways and means by which this indebtedness shall be met." Thus the old story was resumed and to add to its volume, a committee was then appointed to take steps towards erecting sheds.

September 16th it was resolved "That a special collection be taken up for foreign missions the first Sabbath in October, and one for the benefit of the widows and orphans of deceased ministers the third Sabbath." It was further proposed to take up a special collection from church members " to meet arrears in incidental expenses."

October 4th—Previous to the communion Bro. and Sister Havens, also their son and daughter, were received by letter from the St. Catharines Church, and Jabez Montgomery from Ann Arbor, Mich. On the Wednesday following it was resolved " That this church do cordially invite the Baptist Missionary Convention of Ontario to meet here next year.

On the 28th of October Thomas Johnston, E. W. Dadson and S. L. Head related their Christian experience and were received as members after baptism. Rev. C. Perin and wife, from Dorchester, and Rev. J. Crawford and wife, from Cheltenham, put in their letters, and were received as members. A license to preach was granted to Bro. Baird.

November 18th, 1868, Bro. J. A. Northrup and J. A. Baldwin and wife were received by letter. It was voted, "to pay out of the church treasury the sum of $2 to the home mission fund." Surely this was "the day of small things." At this meeting the ladies were asked to hold a teameeting about Christmas Day "To aid in paying for the church sheds now in course of erection."

November 24th Mrs. Burtch reported that the ladies had decided to hold such teameeting, and asked for committees to assist them in the work—which was done.

Sabbath, December 6th, the pastor gave the hand of fellowship to Neil McCallum and wife and two daughters, T. Johnston, E. W. Dadson and S. L. Head.

It may be said, here, that this was an eventful year and rich in the ingathering of souls. Large numbers were added to the church roll by letter and by baptism; many from the college, and some of whom changed their life plans and became ministers in God's service, and are still doing valiant work in His vineyard.

A special church meeting was held January 22nd, 1869, when the annual report from the treasurer was received, and auditors appointed to audit the same "That the sum of $53, balance in hand in the poor fund, be applied to incidental expenses." At a subsequent meeting this was changed to "a loan."

Committees were appointed to collect for the "Auxiliary Home Mission Society."

Pastor Bates was requested to retire, when Dr. Fyfe was appointed chairman, and resolutions were passed deciding to give the pastor a donation on Thursday evening next, to be held in the basement; and committees appointed to assure success.

No further mention is made in regard to this matter, but it is safe to infer that it was duly carried out.

March 17th Bro. A. E Willis asked the privilege of using the basement once a month for the purpose of holding socials to raise funds for the benefit of the Sabbath School—granted.

Bro. and Sister Caswell received letters to unite with the Pictou church, N. S.; C. Perrin and wife to Georgetown, and Bro. Northrup to Port Burwell.

Church meeting, May 19th—Revs. Dr. Fyfe and Dr. Crawford were appointed delegates to the Springford Church, to examine in council C. W. Haycock, and, if found advisable, ordain him to the gospel ministry.

Brethren Fyfe, Pavey, Havens, Crawford, Bates and Carryer were appointed delegates to the association, to be held at Waterford, and the pastor and clerk prepare statistics.

June 16th, 1869, S. S. Bates, Miss Martha Head, and Miss E. A. Crawford related their Christian experience before the church and were admitted for baptism and church membership.

It was voted to grant $5 to the treasurer of the " Red River Fund."

A question was raised as to the grant of the church to A. E. Willis of the use of the basement, as an individual, when it was decided that the grant was to the young people of the church, and not to Bro. Willis.

On Sabbath evening, June 20th, the pastor baptized J. I. Bates, S. S. Bates, E. A. Crawford, M. Head and E. McDermid; and on July 4th, they, with C. Braham and W. Monkman, received the hand of fellowship.

CHAPTER IX.

A Great Storm—Baptist Convention—Designation of John Mc-
Laurin for the Mission Field—Enlargement of the Church
—Weekly Offering System—First Paid Organist—Jubilee
Services—Re-opening— Young People's Society— Resigna-
tion of Elder Bates.

August 18th Brethren Fyfe, Crawford and Topping were appointed delegates to the St. Mary's church to ordain E. D. Sher-
man to the ministry. At this meeting an account was presented
for glass and glazing windows, broken by the great hail storm
in June last.

It might be mentioned, in explanation, that the storm referred
to was the most severe ever known in this town. It occurred
on Sunday afternoon ; and such was its violence that no exposed
window escaped : and there was not glass enough in stock in
Woodstock to repair damages. Persons or animals exposed to
the immense hailstones received great injury therefrom, and the
streets were flooded to a large extent.

September 15th committees were appointed to make all necessary arrangements for holding the convention, " that would be
creditable to church and congregation." No mention is made in
the minutes ; but we have other records to show that it was one
of the most enthusiastic meetings ever held by the denomination.
The most interesting exercise was the designation of Bro. John
McLaurin as missionary-elect for India. Two years ago Bro
Timpany was set apart at that " wonderful " meeting held in Ingersoll ; but, if possible, the enthusiasm at this meeting was even
greater. Mr. McLaurin reported the results of his 4,000 miles
travel in behalf of the missions in Ontario and Quebec, and
which kindled a missionary zeal such as never before experienced ; and which afterward culminated in establishing a foreign

mission of our own among the Telugus, with Bro. McLaurin as first missionary.

At the church meeting, November 24th, the pastor's salary was raised to $700, beginning the 1st of January, 1870, and arrangements made for a social and donation in January.

January 19th, 1870, J. E. Wells and R. H. Burtch were appointed auditors.

The pastor presented a letter to the church, urging the propriety of enlarging the building. A committee was appointed to take the matter into consideration.

At the monthly meeting, 16th February, the report of the committee on enlargement of the chapel was received and discussed, the committee discharged, and a new one appointed to circulate a subscription list.

March 2nd Bro. S. L. Head was granted a license to preach the gospel.

The building committee was authorised to proceed with the enlargement and the erection of a new fence. The trustees were also authorized to borrow $1,000 to apply on the payment of such improvements.

Among others, receiving the hand of fellowship on the 6th of March, was J. W. A. Stewart ; D. W. Karn was received on the 16th, by letter from Beachville.

April 24th the pastor, Dr. Fyfe, and brethren Cox and Sawtell were delegated to sit in council in Brantford for the purpose of recognizing a 2nd Baptist Church there. The pastor baptized twelve the same evening.

A special meeting was called on the 11th May to discuss plans and costs of improvements, but resulted in no definite action. It was agreed to give due notice and discuss the matter more fully on the 18th instant.

May 18th Elder Bates was appointed to write the circular letter to the association, to be held in Springford, and Brethren J. I. Bates, W. Pavey, R. A. Fyfe, E. Topping and J. Midgley, delegates. It was resolved " That the building committee be requested to modify the plans, so as to reduce the cost, and report next meeting."

May 25th a report was submitted, with plans, estimated to cost $1,300, fully discussed, adopted,and the committee instructed to proceed at once.

June 15th the trustees reported that they would be obliged to dispose of three acres of the new cemetery, to meet liabilities and erect new fences—left in their hands to do as circumstances dictated.

Elder Bates and Dr. Fyfe were appointed delegates to Galt, to assist in organizing and recognizing a Baptist Church there.

July 27th the building committee reported "That they could not get the improvements proposed at the cost estimated, and recommended that on account of putting the work so late in the fall, the matter be laid over till the following spring, asking the subscribers to honor their subscriptions then." The report of the building committee was adopted.

August 17 Dr. Fyfe was delegated to attend the ordination of Bro. George Samis at West Flamboro.

October 19th Brethren Crawford and Topping were appointed delegates to a council in East Zorra Church, to ordain Brother H. Bolton to the ministry.

December 4th the pastor and Bro. Cox were delegated to sit in council at Waterdown, to recognize a Baptist Church there.

December 21st a resolution was passed calling a general conference meeting of the church and congregation, to be held on the second Thursday in January, 1871, to consider matters of interest.

The meeting referred to was held, and an interesting discussion of church affairs took place, resulting in the recommendation of the adoption of the weekly offering system for the raising of general funds A committee was appointed to bring in a re-report of a plan at next meeting.

January 18th, 1871, collectors were appointed to canvass for funds for the home missions.

It was resolved "That the control of the singing and playing upon the instrument be entirely under the direction of the church."

"That R. W. Sawtell and W. Pavey be the music committee for this year."

The committee on the weekly offering system reported a plan, which was adopted, and R. W. Sawtell and W. Nasmyth appointed a committee to carry it out.

February 1st, 1871, the music committee recommended the appointment of Miss Bell as organist, at the salary of $30 per annum—report adopted. This is the first official appointment of an organist and cannot be considered an extravagant salary. It was sufficient, however, to commit the church to the principal, and is also an indication that the organ had come to stay—notwithstanding the strong prejudice of some, who, on account of this action, left the church.

May 7th the delegates to the association were the pastor, E. Topping, J. Hatch, E. Miller, C. Herrington—J. E. Wells to write the circular letter.

A resolution was passed to take up a collection to pay the expenses of the delegates.

October 11th the question of enlargement was again discussed, and a new building committee, consisting of Brethren Sawtell, Hatch, Biggins, Nasmyth, H. T. Burtch and F. B. Schofield appointed.

The canvassing committee was urged to secure promises for at least $1,500, payable 1st of April and 1st November, 1872.

Mr. Judd White was appointed leader of the choir.

December 27th W. Nasmyth tendered his resignation of the offices of treasurer and trustee. A resolution of appreciation of his services was passed.

Dr. Fyfe, R. H. Burtch and R. W. Sawtell were appointed a committee to convey the thanks of the church to him. They, at the same time, presented him with a writing desk.

R. W. Sawtell was then elected trustee in place of James Cox, who had resigned, and instructed to collect arrearages on lots sold in the cemetery.

February 21st, 1872, six members of the Reddick family were received by letters as members.

At this meeting it was resolved "That we hold jubilee services in this Church on the 22nd of April; and that the following be a committee to carry out the arrangements for the same, viz.: Messrs. Pavey, Sawtell, R.H. Burtch, Biggins, Hatch, Nasmyth, H. F. Burtch, Dr. Howland and the pastor; also Mrs. Hatch, Mrs. Pavey, Mrs. A. Burtch, Mrs. Sawtell, Mrs. Wells and Mrs. Carryer."

March 3rd the pastor and Deacon Pavey were appointed delegates to a council at Galt, to ordain George Wheeler if deemed advisable.

No further mention is made of the jubilee; but other records remind us that it was an event of great interest to the church.

On Sabbath, April 21, Dr. Fyfe preached an eloquent discourse in the forenoon, and Rev. W. Stewart—then of Bond street, Toronto—in the evening. The building was crowded at each service, and good collections given in aid of the building fund.

On Monday evening, April 22nd, a soiree was held. Tea was served from six to eight o'clock, after which the large assembly was addressed by several former pastors and others. Mr. Landon read an historical sketch of the early days of the church, and exhibited a model, built with logs, of the schoolhouse where the church was organized and worshipped for many years.

A committee was subsequently appointed to have the "sketch and Dr. Fyfe's sermon printed"; but it was never done. It was afterwards lodged in the college museum.

The jubilee choir of the church was led by John Weeks, and the drilling, then received, placed it in frequent demand by the Y. M. C. A. and other organizations for some time thereafter. R. W. Sawtell was appointed leader.

May 15th Brethren R. H. Burtch, E. Miller, E. Topping, C. Bradley, W. Pavey and the pastor were appointed delegates to the association—to be held at Burgessville—the pastor to write the circular letter.

Dr. Fyfe, J. Crawford and E Topping were delegated to meet in council with the Burgessville Church on July 25th, to ordain W. D. Lowther.

The enlargement of the church was proceeded with immediately after the jubilee services. It consisted in extending the back wall 16 feet to the boundary of the lot on the north, with a wing on the east and west, giving one extra exit by a door in the east and a choir gallery and door in the west wing.

November 10th, 1872, a reopening of the chapel took place with Rev. A. H. Munro, of Toronto, at 11 a. m., Rev. C. Perrin, of Georgetown, at 6.30 p. m. Appropriate addresses were given to the Sabbath school in the afternoon.

On Monday evening a platform meeting was, held when addresses were given by several good speakers, and the choir gave some choice renderings.

November 13th, a vote of thanks was passed and tendered to the trustees of the Institute for the use of their chapel "during the time the contractors had possession of our own place of worship."

The trustees were requested to erect a picket fence along the east and south sides of the property. It was resolved "That the church pay pew rent in advance to commence from the present quarter."

The weekly offering system presented by the committee did not obtain favor at this time, and fell through.

January 15th, 1873, Bro. Clifford resigned the office of deacon of the church—resignation accepted.

The treasurer presented his annual statement. D. W. Karn and R. W. Sawtell were appointed auditors.

In order to bring the work of the Sabbath School more into touch with the church, it was resolved " That as the work of the Sabbath School instruction is recognized as part of the church's work, and ought to be encouraged by it, we hold a social tea-meeting here on Thursday, 23rd instant, for the benefit of its funds."

Collectors were appointed " to procure funds for the missionary convention."

February 19th C. C. Carryer wished to be relieved from being a member of the finance committee, which was done.

Bro. John Hatch was unanimously elected deacon of the church.

March 19th Brethren Montgomery and Biggins were duly elected deacons.

April 6th—A series of weekly meetings had been held by the pastor and very large numbers "brought to the Light," and presented themselves for baptism. At no time in the history of the church had there been such an interest, or as many converted to the truth.

At this meeting we find the following resolution inserted, which evinces the tenacity to which some hold a prejudice against the "innovation of instrumental music" moved by E. Topping, March 9th, and lost; but, by his request, was now inserted in the minutes :

"Whereas Bro. James Martin has been for a number of years grieved on account of the manner in which instrumental music was introduced into this church ; and whereas he now expresses his willingness to be reconciled to the church, on condition that the church passes a resolution expressing regret that instrumental music was introduced in such a manner as to grieve any of its members ; thererefore, resolved, That this church does regret that it should have been so introduced as to grieve or give offence to any brother or sister."

Sabbath, May 4th, was a day long to be remembered. The hand of fellowship was given by Pastor Bates to 24 new members, nearly all of whom had been recently baptized—18 were females and 6 males.

Revs. Bates and Fyfe and Deacon Pavey were delegated to sit in council at Petrolea on the ordination of Bro. Johnston.

May 21st Brethren Fyfe, Pavey, Karn, McCall and the pastor were appointed to attend as delegates to the association, to be held at Villa Nova—pastor and R. W. Sawtell to write the circular letter.

Sunday, May 25th, eight were baptized.

June 18th the young people of the church, having organised

E

themselves into a society known as the "Young People's Christian Association in connection with the church," and desiring to establish a Sabbath School in the west end of the town, reported that they proposed to buy a lot, and asked the liberty to have the deed made to the trustees of this church—request granted.

A letter was read from the pastor, resigning his charge of the pastorate.

Special church meeting held 25th June. The resignation of Bro. Bates was fully discussed ; after which the following resolution was passed : "That while we cannot urge our beloved pastor to continue labors to which he finds his physical strength no longer equal, we cannot permit the peaceful and loving relations we have so long sustained to each other, as pastor and people, to be discontinued without expressing our grateful sense of the fervent piety, intense zeal for our spiritual welfare, and whole-hearted consecration to his Master's work, which have constantly abounded in his labors amongst us ; and we rejoice to be assured that his resignation, at this time, is due to no feeling of dissatisfaction with the imperfect manner in which we have discharged our duties, as a Christian church. In accepting this resignation, we sincerely hope that a release from the arduous labors and responsibilities, necessarily devolving upon the pastor of so large a church, will fully restore his health ; and that we may still enjoy the pleasure of his company and receive the benefit of his mature knowledge and large Christian experience."

The clerk was instructed to send the letter of the pastor and a copy of this resolution to "The Baptist" for publication.

No pastor could be more beloved by his people than Elder Bates ; and never did any pastor work more devoutly and conscientiously for his church—faithful sowing : and abundant reaping was the result. The large accessions to the church, and particularly of the young, gave evidence of his loving ministrations. Nor did it end with his pastorate ; his successor reaped largely, for a year or more, as the results of Mr. Bates' faithful sowing.

Not in the church only were his labors abundant ; but he gave of his means, and his valuable services as secretary of the executive committee of the Institute for many years. In India, also, his name—and those of his two honored daughters, Mrs. Timpany and Mrs. McLaurin—are known and highly honored in many Christian homes as faithful servants of the Lord. In fact he was the faithful advocate and helper in all our denominational enterprizes.

CHAPTER X.

E. W. DADSON LICENSED TO PREACH—CALL TO REV. E. GOODSPEED—INSTALLATION—MISSION SCHOOLS EAST AND WEST—FALL OF CHURCH CEILING—COMMITTEES FOR CHURCH WORK—DEATH OF ELDER BATES—NEW BUILDING ON VANSITTART AVENUE—D. A. McGREGOR.

February 18th, 1874, E. W. Dadson applied to the church for a certificate of recommendation to the work of the Gospel ministry. Letter granted.

Brethren Montgomery, Pavey and Sawtell were appointed a committee to provide a leader of the choir, to succeed the latter, who retired from the leadership.

The committee appointed to nominate a suitable pastor for the church reported in favor of the Rev. Calvin Goodspeed, of New Brunswick.

The report was adopted, and a call forwarded. One thousand dollars per annum was the sum fixed for salary.

March 18th a letter was read from Mr. Goodspeed, accepting the position of pastor, "services to commence 1st of September next."

It was reported, that after paying $40 for wood, $60 towards the new fence and $17.50 towards the organist's salary, the

Ladies' Aid Association intended discontinuing its operations during the summer months. The report was adopted.

Brethren Karn, Sawtell and Howland were appointed a committee to provide accommodation for those who desire to attend the public meeting, to be held at the C. L. Institute, April 7th.

Letters of dismission were granted to Elder Bates and wife, to unite with the church at St. George, where he had accepted a call to the pastorate. Thus, on the 29th day of April, a pastorate (of six years' duration) was severed, which had been greatly blessed of God in the salvation of many souls, and the uplifting of church work and Christian privileges in the church at Woodstock ; surpassing any similar period in its history.

For two years a Sabbath School had been successfully held in the west end, and Mr. Bates, with others, had made efforts to secure a suitable lot for the erection of a school, but so far without success.

July 15th W. Nasmyth resigned the treasurership of the church, and Bro. T. S. McCall was appointed his successor. R. H. Burtch and R. W. Sawtell to audit the late treasurer's books.

October 14th John M. Whyte, who had for some time been leader of the choir, resigned ; and a vote of thanks was tendered him for his efficient services.

The deacons, who had been asked to make arrangements for installation services, reported in favor of holding such meeting on Tuesday evening next.

A committee, previously appointed, submitted a scheme for systematic church work, under the control and charge of the church. It embraced the Sabbath School work, tract distribution, visiting sick, caring for strangers, visiting delinquent members and several other matters. The scheme was adopted, and committees appointed to carry out the various departments of work.

October 20th—The installation of Pastor Goodspeed took place this evening, when Dr. Castle preached an eloquent sermon appropriate to the occasion. Rev. W. H. Porter, of Brantford, gave the address to the pastor ; the right hand of fellowship by the Rev. Dr. Cooper, of London ; the Rev. John Bates, the induction prayer ; and Dr. Fyfe offered the welcome on behalf of the church. The pastor briefly responded and closed by prayer.

November 18th Mr. J. J. Baker was appointed leader of the the choir, in place of Mr. J. M. Whyte, resigned.

Deacon Pavey made a report of the work of the convention, to which he had been a delegate, and stated that he had pledged the church for $50 towards the support of an evangelist for the weak churches.

It was resolved to raise the sum by private subscription.

Sunday, November 22nd, seven candidates were baptized.

December 6th Rev. John Crawford gave the hand of fellowship to Mr. and Mrs. Goodspeed, on their letters from New Brunswick ; after which Pastor Goodspeed gave the hand of fellowship to eight new members.

December 16th the salary of the organist, Mrs. Peers, was fixed at $50 per annum. A new pipe organ had been constructed by D. W. Karn & Co. and placed in the choir gallery.

Dr. Fyfe, J. Montgomery and the pastor were appointed a committee to advise and provide a suitable hymn book for general adoption and use of the church.

January 21st, 1875, Dr. Fyfe reported on behalf of the committee, recommending the adoption of the "Canadian Baptist Hymn Book." Brethren Sawtell and Karn to be the committee to procure them on the best terms possible.

Reports from the east end and west end Sabbath Schools were given, showing very satisfactory results.

R. W. Sawtell reported, on the part of the auditors, that they had discovered an error, in the late treasurer's account, of $100 ; but it was against himself, and Brother Nasmyth forbid the auditors to make it known to the church, or refuses to accept it if the church offers to repay the same.

Sabbath, January 31st, Rev. C. Goodspeed baptised seven candidates at Strathallan, in the forenoon, and sixteen in the Woodstock Church in the evening. The house was crowded.

The centre piece and part of the plaster fell from the ceiling. Fortunately, no one was hurt, but considerable damage was done to the seats. The trustees met on Tuesday morning and decided to recommend the putting up of a substantial wood ceiling.

February 5th a request was made for delegates to sit in council at Strathallan, with the view of organizing a church there. Brethren Pavey, Hatch, Yule, Topping and the pastor were elected delegates thereto.

Letters of dismission were given to twelve members to assist in forming said church.

A plan for a board ceiling, prepared by Mr. Biggins, was submitted to the church and adopted.

Sabbath, 7th February, the hand of fellowship was given to twenty-two members.

February 17th—Moved by R. W. Sawtell, seconded by T. S. McCall, "That, whereas this church is indebted to the late treasurer, W. Nasmyth, $100, being an error in the building fund account—and the costs of the new ceiling amounting to $350, requiring the total sum of $450—therefore : " Resolved, That a committee be appointed to raise the amount by special subscription."

Sabbath day, March 14, the ceiling having been completed, the church returned to its own audience room, and Dr. Fyfe preached an excellent sermon. Prof Crawford baptised seven candidates for Gobles Church. In the evening Pastor Good speed preached and baptised 21 candidates.

March 17 Bro. Cull resigned the office of deacon.

The music committee were requested to confer with Mr. Karn as to the cost of the small pipe organ erected by the company.

It was also decided to hold a social in favor of the Sabbath School.

Almost every Sabbath evening through the winter candidates were baptised, and on the 4th of April the pastor gave the hand of fellowship to forty-seven members—the largest number in the the history of the church on one Sabbath. Among those admitted by letter was Dr. McLay. Nearly all the candidates baptised were young people, and to-day very many of them are the active members of the church.

April 21 J. I. Bates was appointed superintendent of the Sabbath School.

Brethren Sawtell, Karn, McLay and W. Clarke were appointed to select a site for a west end mission school.

Karn, Sawtell and Nasmyth, a committee to billet friends attending a meeting at the Institute.

May 19th a letter from Bro. John McLaurin was read, asking aid for foreign missions.

Delegates to the association : T. S. McCall, J. Hatch, C. Clarke, R. H. Burtch and the pastor ; Prof. Wells and clerk to write the letter.

A new scheme was submitted to manage the finances—under a financial committee consisting of the deacons, trustees and treasurer—dividing the church into sections, and soliciting aid from every member personally ; enjoining the duty of each one giving something ; and anyone six months in arrears for pew rent, such seat "to revert to the church." The report was accepted, discussed and adopted.

Sabbath, June 6th, Dr. Fyfe gave the hand of fellowship to eight new members.

June 23rd a report was read from the Ladies' Aid Society, which was adopted, and a vote of thanks tendered for material aid rendered to the finances of the church.

R. W. Sawtell presented a report of the cemetery fund and referred to the action of the Credit Valley Railway Company requiring part of the cemetery. A vote of thanks was given him, and he was requested to look well to the interests of this church, in regard to the right of way referred to. It was afterwards arbitrated for and 2½ acres sold.

R. H. Burtch was elected deacon in place of Bro. Cull, resigned.

Sunday, August 1st, Dr. Fyfe preached and gave the hand of fellowship to a number of new members.

Bro. Goodspeed's hea'th having given way, under the strain of heavy work all winter, the church voted him a month's vacation "for a rest and to recruit his health."

September 16 the resignation of W. H. Bradley as sexton was accepted, and Bro. Clifford appointed to that position.

October 21st Bro. Nasmyth's resignation as trustee was accepted, and a vote of thanks tendered him. On November 18th E. H. Grove was elected trustee.

After a short season of rest Mr. Bates, our late pastor, accepted the pastorate of the St. George Church, and was there only about a year, when, after a very short illness, he was called away "to everlasting bliss" on the 8th day of October, 1875, and was buried in the Woodstock Baptist cemetery.

December 16th Mrs. Sarah Bates was received by letter from the St. George Church, and Brother and Sister Landon "by experience."

At the first meeting in January, 1876, Bro John Torrance was received by letter from the Yorkville Church.

A vote of thanks was passed in favor of Bro. T. S. McCall for "very able services rendered as treasurer of the church."

February 24, 1876, a special church meeting was held. R. W. Sawtell gave a verbal report from the finance committee, in reference to the debt on the church and the need of accommodation for the west end school, requiring about $3,300. He then moved, That an effort be made to raise $1,000 by subscription this year, in two payments, to provide accommodation for the Sabbath School in the west end ; provided that $200 of the same be applied to the debt on the church." Carried unanimously.

The matter was left in the hands of the finance committee, who were to submit plans and estimates to the church.

It was also decided to hold a social on the following Monday evening for the benefit of the Sabbath School—twenty cents admission.

Sabbath, March 5th, ten members received the hand of fellowship.

Special meeting, April 27th. The canvassing committee reported subscriptions to the amount of $998 as pledges for the new school house, to be erected on the corner of Hunter street and Vansittart avenue, where a corner lot had been selected. The tender for the building was awarded to Bickerton & Co., for the sum of $875. Reports adopted.

May 18th Bro. Carryer resigned the office of deacon. On motion it was accepted, and Mr. Carryer thanked for his services.

R. W. Sawtell reported proposed terms of union with the Presbyterian brethren in regard to management of cemeteries— adopted.

The finance committee was authorised to borrow $600 "to meet financial requirements."

Delegates to the association : Brethren Goodspeed, Montgomery, Bates, J. Topping and McCall ; the pastor and Montgomery to write the letter.

June 14th the pastor and brethren Topping and Karn were delegated to sit in council with the Beachville Church, for the purpose of ordaining J. W. A. Stewart.

D. W. Karn was elected deacon in place of C. C. Carryer, resigned.

August 24th a license was granted to Bro. T. S. McCall to "improve his gifts" in preaching the gospel.

The west end mission chapel was duly opened, and preaching once a Sabbath by students and others established.

The trustees were authorised to erect a gate and fence the cemetery with wire fence.

August 31 instructions were given the trustees to have gaslight introduced into the church at a cost of $70.

A Sabbath School picnic was authorized to be held on the 4th of September.

Brethren Grove, Sawtell and R. H. Burtch were elected a music committee.

Father Hallam and J. H. Hill were admitted members, and on the 23rd of November E. W. Dadson was dismissed by letter to the Denfield Church.

The hour for preaching in the west end was changed to 6.30 p.m.

Sunday, January 7th, 1877, the hand of fellowship was given to seven members.

Sunday, February 4th, ten members were admitted to membership.

February 22nd the committee having the charge of the west end mission reported that they had subscriptions to the amount of $80, and recommended the appointment of D. A. McGregor to the charge of the mission for six months.

March 1st—At a special meeting the weekly offering system was again discussed, and the deacons requested to report thereon at next meeting.

It was decided to have a "basket social" to raise funds for the Sabbath School on the 13th.

March 15th it was resolved to adopt the free seat and weekly offering systems.

April 18th Pastor Goodspeed, Dr. Fyfe and Deacon Burtch were delegated to attend a council at Salford, to recognize a Baptist church there.

Special church meeting March 29th—A lengthy report from the deacons was adopted, referring to a plan to liquidate the debt ; to make other improvements ; resignation of Bro. Biggins as treasurer and appointment of Bro. J. H. Bache, and E. H. Groves as assistant treasurer and collector of weekly offerings ; appointment of T. S. McCall, A. O. McKee and R. G. Sawtell as ushers ; a vote of thanks to the Ladies' Aid Society for the sum of $100 for gas fitting fund. A vote of thanks was passed in favor of Bro. Biggins for services as treasurer.

April 1 the pastor gave the hand of fellowship to thirteen new members, including G. B. Davis and D. Lang by letters.

Bro. Torrance gave notice that at the next meeting he would make a motion to elect all officers annually, by ballot, including the two senior deacons.

The delegates appointed to attend the association at Simcoe were : the pastor, T. S. McCall, R. A. Fyfe, J. Hatch and R. H. Burtch. The beneficent card plan for missions was introduced ; Brethren McKee and Bache appointed to carry out the system.

July 19th various reports were read from committees appointed to visit delinquent members, with the view of revising the church roll. Some promised better attendance for the future, and some names were dropped from the roll—including W. Nasmyth, whose case had been under consideration of the church for years; having been labored with under the advice of various committees, but all failed to reconcile him on supposed grievances.

The pastor was granted a month's vacation.

November 1st Brethren Hatch and Torrance were appointed to sit in council at the Burgessville Church to examine and ordain Bro. Munroe.

November 15 Bro. Montgomery asked to be relieved from deaconship on account of press of work. The church declined to accept his resignation, and urged him to continue.

December 6th—At the request of the Adelaide Street Baptist Church, London, a delegation, consisting of the pastor, Bro. Torrance, Bro. Karn and Bro. Catling, was sent to sit in council, for the purpose of recognizing said church.

January 17th, 1878, a member of the church brought a charge against the members for non-attendance at the funeral of his six months old child; whereupon a resolution of "condolence and sympathy for the parents was passed."

A committee was appointed to promote greater sociability among the members, consisting of Montgomery, Sawtell, Bache, Pavey, McKee and Raymer.

January 24th the treasurer's report was read, and the thanks of the church tendered to Bro. Bache for the very satisfactory manner in which the work had been done. Also a vote of thanks to the auditors.

February 3 the social committee reported in favor of forming a "mutual improvement association" and meeting periodically. To hold the first after-tea social on the following Friday evening—adopted.

February 21st it was resolved: (1) "That this church adopts the "Baptist Church Manual"—as the rules of order, and "Declaration of Faith," and that the clerk be instructed to purchase

one hundred copies for distribution among the members.
(2) That one hundred copies of Sanky and Bliss' "Sacred Songs
and Solos" be purchased for the use of the prayer meetings, and
twenty-five copies for use in the gaol services. (3) That the following be officers of the "Mutual Improvement Society," viz :
E. H. Grove, pres.; R. G. Sawtell, vice-pres.; A. O. McKee, sec.;
F. H. Muir, treas."

The friends of temperance asked for the use of the church on
the 11th of March to hold a meeting therein—granted.

March 3rd Bro. Challen, who had been conducting the singing for some time, tendered his resignation; but was asked by
the church to reconsider the matter.

The treasurer and his assistant were re-elected for another
year.

May 16th Rev. C. Goodspeed, Dr. Fyfe, W Pavey, T. S. Mc-
Call and J. Hatch were appointed delegates to attend the association at Vittoria ; T. S. McCall, R. W. Sawtell and the clerk
to write the circular letter.

Bro. Bache having resigned the treasurership, on account of
leaving, Bro. D. W. Karn was appointed treasurer.

A resolution of regret, to see Bro. Bache leave the town, and
expressive of the appreciation of his services while a member of
this church, was passed, and a committee appointed to give some
tangible expression of our regards for himself and wife.

This was done, and an address and presentation made, before
his departure for the "Old Country."

CHAPTER XI.

Rev. C. Goodspeed Resigns—Annual Elections of Deacons Initi-
ated—Death of Dr. Fyfe—Beneficent Card Plan—Call to
Rev. Mr. Johnston—Declined—Rev. J. Torrance Supplies—
Rev. B. F. Ashley Accepts a Call—Bro. Wells' Resignation
—Closing the West Mission—Death of Prin. Torrance.

June 20th Pastor Goodspeed read before the meeting his
resignation as pastor.

Special meeting held July 2nd—Prof. Torrance in the chair.
There was a full meeting of members. The resignation of Pastor Goodspeed was read, and after some discussion and a full
explanation by the deacons, Bro. Montgomery moved the following resolution : "That in accepting the resignation of our
pastor, Rev. C. Goodspeed, M. A., we desire to express our
appreciation of him as an earnest, faithful and devoted minister
of the gospel, believing, as we do, that he is a 'workman that
needeth not to be ashamed, rightly dividing the word of truth';
and further resolved, That we extend to him, wherever God's
Providence may place him in the future, our best wishes, our
sympathies and our prayers ; and that a vacation of four weeks
be given to Bro. Goodspeed." "That the deacons be constituted
a supply committee, and also to make arrangements for the
settlement of a pastor."

At this time the deacons pressed their resignation upon the
church, when, after some explanation, it was Resolved, "That
the question of electing deacons annually be laid upon the
table until next church meeting.

"Resolved, That the limit of salary for the pastor be recon-
sidered and opened for discussion at next meeting."

July 8th, Bro. Torrance in the chair. The following resolutions were passed : "That the previous salary of the pastor be
a sufficient guide to the committee." "That the trustees be

elected annually, on the first regular business meeting in January, and two retire annually thereafter." "That the deacons be elected in the same way." "That they be requested to withdraw their resignations now before the church.'" "That the finance committee pay three months' rent for East end Sabbath school room."

That the week-night prayer meeting be held on Wednesday evening, instead of Thursday evening.

August 4th, a delegation, consisting of Brethern Pavey, Topping and Karn, were appointed to sit in council at the Bayham church, on a matter of dispute between the pastor and the deacons there.

It is not a part of this work to chronicle the death of the ministers; but it would be remiss to omit a reference to such a benefactor as Dr. Fyfe.

In 1865 he had been attending the Baptist anniversaries in St. Louis, Missouri, and while returning a collision occurred, which overturned the car he was in, and which so affected his nervous system that he never fully recovered from the shock. This, added to the worries of financial deficits and college labors, gradually overcame his powerful physique and robust constitution. He gradually failed, and on the 4th of September, 1878, passed away to higher duties and greater responsibilities.

His remains were taken to Toronto, and buried by the side of his first wife, in the Necropolis. Thus passed from our church life one of the wisest counsellors, truest friend, liberal giver and ablest preacher this or any other church ever had, and it may be truly said, "We shall never see his like again."

October 23rd, Bro. George McKee received a letter of dismission to the Orangeville church. J. E. Vining, E. Hazleton and wife, and N. Wolverton were received by letter.

Bro. Chute gave a verbal report of the state of the East Sabbath school, asking for help.

R. W. Sawtell, who had for some time led the choir, resigned, and was thanked by the church for past services; and Bro. E. H. Grove appointed to take his place.

Sunday, December 1st, Rev. J. Torrance gave the hand of fellowship to J. H. Kennedy, A. Dewar ; and F. W. Avauche received a letter to the Galt church.

December 11th—On motion of Dr. McLay and D. W. Karn, Professor Watt was engaged for three months for the sum of $50, to train the choir and members of the congregation in singing.

January 15th, 1879—It was resolved, That the scheme proposed for the more efficient working of the beneficent card plan be adopted, and a committee appointed to carry it out.

January 16th—Trustees were elected as follows: For three years, W. Pavey and R. H. Burtch; two years, R. W. Sawtell and E. H. Grove: one year, John Hatch and W. Biggins.

Deacons—For three years, Biggins and Pavey; two years, Burtch and Hatch; one year, Karn and Grove. Treasurer, D. W. Karn: Assistant, E. H. Grove; Clerk, C. C. Carryer: Ushers—W. Chave and W. Duncan.

January 29th—Resolved, To hold a tea-meeting in February, for the benefit of the Sabbath school, the teachers to be the committee of arrangement; fee, 25 cents.

Brethern Hunter and Torrance were delegated to sit in council at Port Rowan over some church difficulties.

February 19th—The beneficent card system, as recommended by circular, was adopted, and Bro. F. Muir appointed superintendent of the same.

Reports from the east and west mission Sabbath schools were read and adopted, and the superintendents sustained in their work.

March 19th, Deacon Montgomery reported, on behalf of the supply committee, in favor of giving a call to the Rev. Mr. Johnston, of the Eastern States, who had acceptably supplied the pulpit the last two Sabbaths.

It was moved by R. W. Sawtell, chairman of the finance committee, seconded by W. Pavey, that a call to the pastorate of this church be extended to the Rev. Mr. Johnston, and that the vote be taken by ballot.

March 26th—T. S. McCall and R. G. Sawtell were appointed scrutineers, and the vote on the call of the pastor taken by ballot, when it was found that there was 86 for and 10 against.

The sum of $1,000 was fixed for the annual salary, and the expenses of moving were to be paid by the church; and one month's vacation allowed each year.

April 23rd—The supply committee reported that the Rev. Mr. Johnston had failed in getting a release from his present pastorate, hence "could not accept the call so kindly extended to him." Report received, and committee requested to proceed in procuring a pastor.

R. W. Sawtell reported, that in accordance with the terms of the deed of conveyance of the church property, the election of trustees was illegal ; hence the two former trustees, left off in the said election, must be restored and the board remain as before, viz.: Messrs. Pavey, Topping, Carryer, R. H. Burtch, Grove and Sawtell. Report adopted accordingly.

April 30th Bro. Goodspeed gave the hand of fellowship to Miss McKee and Brethren Dayfoot, Weir and Haviland. Dr. McLay and wife returned from the Aylmer church.

May 7th a careful report from the deacons, recommending a revision of the church roll, was adopted and many names of absent and delinquent members dropped from the roll.

Brethren Sawtell and Carryer appointed to write the association letter.

August 3rd Bro. Walker, of Thorold (who supplied the pulpit to-day), and Brethren McQuarrie and Beardsall were appointed delegates to attend a council at Drumbo, for the purpose of ordaining J. D. McCall. The hand of fellowship was given by Bro. Walker to Brethren Watts, Willard, Heath, Geo. Peters and wife.

August 6th Bro. Montgomery reported that he had gathered from private correspondence with Rev. Mr. Johnson that it was possible to obtain his acceptance of the pastorate here if we could afford to advance the salary to $1,200. It was unanimously resolved to make that offer and repeat the call.

Deacon Karn reported that on the recommendation of Rev. Mr. Codville, he had taken upon himself the responsibility of inviting the Rev. Mr. Ashley, of Pittsburg, to supply the pulpit here on the 17th and 24th of August.

August 20th a committee was appointed to prepare an address to Bro. Montgomery and wife, who were intending to return to Ann Arbor, they having rendered twelve years' faithful services to the church.

August 24th the address mentioned was read by the committee and approved by the church.

A resolution was passed to raise the sum of one hundred dollars for the home mission fund.

September 24 Brethren Sawtell and Karn were appointed to audit the books of the superintendent of the "card plan," F. Muir being about to leave for the west. J. Millard was appointed to the position left vacant by his removal.

Rev. Mr. Ashley, having supplied the pulpit for two Sabbaths, and having furnished numerous testimonials speaking in the highest terms of his abilities and piety, it was : Resolved to extend to him a call to the pastorate here at a salary of $1,200 per annum.

October 22nd it was decided to hold a social at which the pastor-elect would be inducted. Committees were appointed to carry out the proceedings.

Sabbath morning, November 2nd, 1879, the Rev. W. H. Landon gave the hand of fellowship to Mr. and Mrs. Ashley and daughter, and Mrs. Harper ; also to Mrs. Wolverton, H. J. Nowland and Miss B. Sinclair.

November 19th R. W. Sawtell reported that the proceeds of the teameeting amounted to $95.75.

The trustees reported in favor of making alterations in the singing gallery.

Mr. Karn reported progress in regard to upholstering the seats—inviting the ladies to assist.

December 17th Mr. Goodspeed was appointed superintendent of the beneficent fund, in place of J. Millard—resigned, and

F

D. W. Karn, S. J. McKee and R. W. Sawtell appointed a committee on socials.

January 29th, 1880, Rev. John McLaurin was received by letter from the Stratford church. Twelve candidates were separately voted on and received for baptism and membership. The following officers were elected, viz : Deacons—D. W. Karn and E. H. Grove ; treasurer, D. W. Karn ; assistant, E. H. Grove ; clerk, C. C. Carryer.

Bro. Topping tendered his resignation as trustee, and was asked to reconsider it.

It was resolved that Brethren Karn, S. J. McKee and Sawtell be appointed to print a list of the members.

Rev. John Torrance and Prof. Goodspeed were appointed delegates to sit in council at Plattsville, to organize and recognize a Baptist church there.

March 7th the hand of fellowship was given to forty new members.

April 4th, eight members received the hand of fellowship from the pastor.

May 19th, the delegates appointed to attend the association at Tilsonburg were the pastor and Brethren Goodspeed, Wolverton, McCall aud Karn.

The statistics and letter, prepared by the clerk, were adopted on June 6th, showing that 47 had been added by baptism, 36 by letter, 2 by experience, and present membership 346.

June 23rd, the pastor and deacons were appointed a standing committee, having supervision over the delinquent members.

The thanks of the church were tendered to Bro. Karn for the use of an organ in the west end mission.

July 21st, A. O. McKee was appointed to superintend the beneficent card plan, in place of Bro. Goodspeed.

September 8th, a special meeting was held to appoint four delegates to the " Canada Baptist Union," to be held in Toronto next month.   The following were elected: R. W. Sawtell, W. Pavey, R. H. Burtch and J. Hatch.

October 6th, the Rev. John Salmon, of the Congregational

church in Embro, made application for baptism, and after giving his experience and explanation was received—also his wife.

Sunday, 14th November, the pastor and Rev. J. Torrance were delegated to attend a council in Toronto, for the purpose of installing Rev. J. Salmon pastor of a Baptist church.

December 19th, H. F. Laflamme, J. S. Hughson, I. S. Foster, and John Washburn were baptized.

December 29th, it was resolved, That all moneys collected for church work be passed through the books of the treasurer, so that a more accurate record may be made.

January 20, 1881, the annual meeting was held, when the following reports were read and adopted: Cemetery, R. W. Sawtell; Treasurer, D. W. Karn; Sabbath school, R. G. Sawtell; East mission, Bro. Weir.

Two deacons were balloted for, resulting in the election of John Hatch and R. H. Burtch. Treasurer and assistant, Karn and Grove. Superintendent of benificent card system, A. O. McKee. It was voted to pay $3.50 per month for rent of mission school-room in the east end.

January 26th, letters of dismission were granted to Bro. J. E. Wells and daughter, to a Toronto church.

Bro. Wells had been a faithful and helpful member of the church for so many years, that it was with profound regret that circumstances had determined him to give up teaching at the college here, and the church felt it keenly.

During the latter years of Dr. Fyfe, and especially after his health became enfeebled, Prof. Wells had been practically the principal, and after the doctor's death Mr. Wells was appointed principal of the literary department, and Rev. J. Torrance principal of the theological.

Bro. Torrance now became principal of the whole school, but symptoms of failing health were evident, and Prof. Torrance's friends feared the worst in his case also.

February 16th, Rev. W. Pickard and family were received by letter by Guelph.

April 13th—For some time it had been found by experience

that a mistake was made in erecting a mission school on Vansittart avenue. During the many years it was held on Dundas street west, the attendance at the Sabbath school was large, and the occasional preaching by the students was well attended, and a deep interest felt.

Prof. McGregor, while in charge of the mission, reported that the present location was not right, and advised opening the Sabbath school where the children were: but there was no response to this appeal, and the result was that the mission was abandoned, and a resolution passed, this evening, to adopt the report of the committee, who had charge of the property, to sell, as they had been offered $900—it had cost the church about double that amount.

May 18th, letters of dismission were given to S. J. McKee and wife, to Manitoba; S. S. Bates, to Goble's; John Trotter, to Strathroy, and George Frazer received by letter from Belleville.

Brethren Ashley, McLaurin and R. H. Burtch, were delegated to sit in council at Goble's, on the ordination of Bro. S. S. Bates, on June 1st.

Brethren D. W. Karn and J. Beardsall to attend a council at Ingersoll on the ordination of D. Hutchinson, their pastor-elect.

The pastor and J. McLaurin to write the letter to the association, and, with Pavey, Hatch, Catling and Beardsall, to attend the association as delegates. The sum of $10 to be sent to the treasurer.

August 7th, the death of Bro. John Torrance was recorded, and it was moved to send a letter of condolence to Mrs. Torrance and family in the deep affliction they were called to endure.

Thus the college was again deprived of a principal, in the very prime of life and mental vigor, and the church of a worthy brother, and as an eloquent, logical and forcible preacher, Bro. Torrance had so earned the entire love and admiration of the church during his frequent ministrations, prior to the coming of Mr. Ashley, that he could have had a unanimous call as its pastor; but he declined; not that he rejected or disliked the work, but that he felt that the call to the work to which he had responded and done so well, as a theological teacher, the more important and necessary.

September 16th, the pastor and deacons Hatch and Pavey were delegated to sit in council in St. George on the ordination of D. H. Mihel.

Letters of dismission were granted to Rev. C Goodspeed and wife—who were leaving the college here, as teachers.

October 4th, Bro. and Sister Westervelt,from Brantford; J.H. Farmer and wife, and Mrs. Springer, from London, teachers-elect at the college, were received on their letters.

December 14th—It was decided to hold a tea-meeting in January next, and a committee appointed to carry it out.

January 19th, 1882, the annual meeting was held this evening, when reports from all departments of church work were received and adopted, and officers elected by ballot as follows :— D. W. Karn, treasurer; C. C. Carryer, clerk; J. Beardsall, assistant treasurer and collector. Beneficent card system, James Catling, superintendent. Deacons, Biggins and Pavey, for three years.

Resolutions were then passed on the following matters: "That the names of all members of whom we have no trace for one year be dropped from the roll." "That the assistant treasurer shall be a member of the finance committee ; that the tea-meeting be held on the 9th of February." "That R. W. Sawtell be empowered to have the constitution and articles of faith and practice printed in pamphlet form." "That the thanks of the church be given to the clerk for services rendered."

March 16th, a report from the deacons advised the dropping a number of names from the church roll for non-attendance and long silent absence. Report adopted.

A license was granted Bro. D. McAlpine to preach, also to Bro. J. Beardsall.

May 17th, the following were appointed delegates to the association to be held at Springford, viz.: The pastor, J. Beardsall, W. Pavey, N. Wolverton, E. Topping, pastor and clerk to prepare the statistics and letter.

Resolved, That the sum of $50 be given to aid in making a sidewalk to the cemeteries, and that Bro. Beardsall be requested to raise it by private subscription.

June 21st, Bro. Robilard was granted a license to preach.

Bro. Pavey tendered his resignation as deacon of the church. Laid on the table.

Bro. Grove tendered his resignation as leader of the choir and deacon of the church. Also laid on the table.

It was resolved that all business meetings close not later than 10 o'clock p. m.

Wednesday, July 19, 1882—In the absence of the pastor, Bro. Wolverton was called to the chair. During the prayer-meeting service Pastor Ashley appeared and spoke at some length, referring to the " present aspect of church matters, and the different private opinions held by church members which affected his position and usefulness here, and expressed his intention to vacate the pulpit and the pastorate of the church." He then left the meeting, when the chairman closed and opened the business meeting.

The minutes were read and adopted. Then a resolution passed rescinding the last one passed at the previous meeting in regard to closing at 10 p. m.

Then the following resolutions were passed: That Deacon Pavey be requested to reconsider his resignation as deacon. That Bro. Grove's resignation as leader of the choir and deacon be accepted.

Moved by E. Topping, seconded by E. Miller, and resolved : " That the resignation of Pastor Ashley, now submitted, be accepted in the most friendly spirit, and the church assures Mr. Ashley that its best wishes for the happiness of himself and family will follow him to wherever God in his Providence may cast his lot.

Moved by W. Pavey, seconded by E. H. Grove, "That a sum equal to one quarter's salary be presented to Mr. Ashley as a friendly offering of the church ; that Brethren Beardsall, Catling and Biggins be the committee on pulpit supply."

August 3rd, a special meeting was called by six members, and N. Wolverton, as chairman, read the same. It was then moved by D. W. Karn, seconded by R. H. Burtch, That, in accordance with the expressed wish of a large representation of the church, contained in a certain requisition, that we deem it expedient for the prosperity of the church, generally, that there be a reorganization of the official board of the church, including the deacons and financial committee. Carried by a count of 38 to 34.

D. W. Karn then tendered his resignation as deacon, and was accepted. R. H. Burtch followed with same result. Bro. Pavey followed, but on a vote being taken his resignation was not accepted. Bro. Beardsall tendered his resignation as assistant-treasurer; not accepted. E. H. Grove resigned as deacon; accepted.

On motion of Deacon Hatch the meeting was then adjourned.

August 16th—J. Beardsall, chairman. The clerk was appointed to write to Dr. Davidson in reference to Bro. McFarlane's letter.

Mrs. Yorke was appointed organist at a salary of $75 per annum.

D. W. Karn appointed leader of the choir.

Scrutineers were appointed and several ballots taken to fill the place of Deacons Karn, Grove and Burtch: but as no one received a two-third vote of the members present, no election took place, and the meeting adjourned.

August 23rd, Rev. G. Richardson and wife were received on their letters.

September 20th, the following were appointed delegates to attend the "Baptist Union," to be held in Hamilton in October, viz.: J. Beardsall, R. W. Sawtell, W. Pavey, J. Catling and R. H. Burtch.

The hour of meeting on Wednesday evenings was changed to 8 p. m.

Letters of dismission were granted to Rev. B. F. Ashley, wife, daughter, and Mrs. Harper, late organist of the church.

Thus ended the connection with the late pastor, during whose

ministrations a large number of members had been added to
the church, and though all things were not always as satisfactory as all could wish, considerable advancement had been made.

The money received from the sale of the west end mission
church was expended in alterations on the Central church,
which greatly improved its appearance, and the accommodation
of the choir and the use of the baptistry.

The election of deacons was again proceeded with, when D.
W. Karn and J. Catling received the required number, and no
others. Adjourned till next regular meeting.

October 2nd, Bro. Richardson in the chair. Balloting for
another deacon was proceeded with, when it was resolved, That
as the ballot failed to procure a three-fourths vote, we defer the
election till the annual meeting in January, 1883.

A committee, consisting of W. H. Landon, G. Richardson,
Beardsall, Catling and Karn, were appointed a committee to prepare a revised draft of the constitution and by-laws.

November 16th, G. Richardson in the chair. Bro. Beardsall
recommended, on the part of the pulpit committee, to corres-
pond with Rev. D. A. McGregor, of Stratford, with a view to a
call to the pastorate of this church. Report adopted, and, with
a view to ascertain the feeling of the meeting in regard thereto,
a vote was taken and found to be entirely unanimous. It was
further decided to submit the question to the church next Sabbath. Salary, $1,000.

November 17th, it was unanimously voted to extend a call to
Bro. McGregor.

December 27th, a letter from Bro. McGregor was read, declining the call to become our pastor.

Letters of dismission were granted to Dr. Crawford and wife,
to unite with the Rapid City church, Man.

The hour of Wednesday evening prayer meeting was fixed at
7:30 for the winter.

January, 17th, 1883, it was decided by an informal vote to extend a call to Dr. Davidson. He came and preached, but the
call at $1,000 was not accepted.

On the following evening the annual meeting was held, Rev. G. Richardson in the chair. Before proceeding with the election of officers, Mr. Karn moved, and R. H. Burtch seconded, that the resolution moved by them, and passed by a small majority at the church meeting, August 3rd, 1882 referring to re-organization of the official board and re-election of officers, be rescinded. Carried unanimously.

The various reports for the past year were then read and adopted. The deacons elected were D. W. Karn and James Catling. Clerk, C. O. Carryer; Karn, treasurer; Beardsall, assistant treasurer; Miss Annie Hatch, organist, Mrs. Yorke having resigned.

Messrs. Karn, Grove and Sawtell were appointed a committee to arrange for an after-tea social to be held February 7th.

It was also decided to hold special evening meetings for prayer during the coming week.

March 28th, a committee was appointed to make arrangements for the entertainment of visitors attending the half-yearly meeting of the board, to be held on the 18th of April.

April 1st, Rev. G. Richardson gave the hand of fellowship to nine new members.

April 19th, Rev. T. S. Johnson, of Sarnia, having preached one Sabbath, was, by a vote of the church, invited to become its pastor.

April 29th, delegates were appointed to attend the "Baptist Union" at Toronto, 1st May, viz.: D. W. Karn, J. Beardsall, J. Hatch, J. H. Hill, W. Pavey and Rev. G. Richardson.

In the evening of the same day Rev. N. Wolverton baptized twenty candidates—chiefly students.

May 9th, a communication was received from Mr. Johnson, expressing regret that he could not accept our call, but thanking the church for its confidence.

May 16th, the following delegates were elected to attend the association, viz.: Brethren Wolverton, Sawtell, Beardsall, Richardson, Topping and R. H. Burtch. The clerk and Mr. Richardson to prepare the letter and statistics.

The delegates were instructed to invite the association to meet in Woodstock next year.

D. W. Karn's resignation as leader of the choir was accepted. It was decided to pay the expenses of the delegates to the association.

A new committee, consisting of J. H. Farmer, D. W. Karn, J. I. Bates, N. Wolverton, J. Beardsall and W. H. Landon were appointed to prepare and submit a draft for a constitution and by-laws.

May 23rd, Sabbath evening services were changed to begin at 7 p. m.

On motion of R. W. Sawtell, seconded by R. H. Burtch, a vote of thanks was tendered to Bro. Karn for his services as leader of the choir.

The statistics at the close of the year, May 31st, showed the number of members to be 325.

July 3rd, a special church meeting was held for the purpose of discussing the draft for constitution and bylaws. Bro. Richardson in the chair, Bro. Sawtell, secretary.

The meeting resolved to go into committee of the whole, and discuss every clause carefully. Four or five nights were given to this matter were finally adopted, and ordered to be printed for the use of the members.

July 10th, the pulpit committee reported in favor of extending a call to Rev. T. Trotter, when it was unanimously voted that a call be given, and that the question be finally disposed of on Sunday next.

Sabbath, July 15th—After preaching by Rev. G. Richardson, he explained the action of the church in regard to the call to Mr. Trotter, and asked for a standing vote of the church. It was unanimous. Prayer by Mr. Landon.

July 18th, Miss A. E. Hatch resigned her position as organist. This was accepted, and the music committee instructed to select and appoint a suitable successor.

July 24, Bro. Trotter met the church this evening to explain his position as student at McMaster Hall, and that he could not take on the full charge of the church for some months. Two weeks were given for further consideration before accepting.

August 15th, a letter was read from Bro. Trotter heartily accepting the charge on the terms proposed.

A vote of thanks was given to Bro. Catling for a present of new gas burners for the pulpit.

On motion of R. W. Sawtell, E. H. Grove was elected leader of the choir.

Brethren Landon, Karn and Grove were appointed a committee to select and recommend a new style of hymn book.

Rev. T. Trotter occupied the pulpit, Sabbath, September 2, as pastor of the church.

Church meeting, September 26th, Pastor Trotter in the chair. The first resolution was to the effect that when the hand of fellowship is withdrawn from any member, the clerk shall notify such member of the fact.

The committee on hymn books recommended the adoption of the Baptist Hymnal.

The report was adopted, and Bro. Karn instructed to order a supply and keep them in stock.

The constitution and by-laws, as amended, were read and finally adopted, and ordered that a pamphlet containing the same, together with an historical sketch of the church, written by Mr. Landon, and the names of the present members, be printed.

Bro. Beardsall was appointed to prepare a letter of condolence from this church to Mrs. Davidson, of Tiverton, on the death of her husband, Dr. Davidson, so long and much respected for his faithful services to the denomination.

A vote of thanks was tendered to Bro. Richardson on his leaving for Toronto, for his kindness in supplying the pulpit so often.

October 17th, Brethren Wolverton and Beardsall were delegated to attend a meeting at Bookton, to appoint an evangelist.

Sabbath, December 2nd, Bro. Landon gave the hand of fellowship to Bro. Trotter. The pastor baptized W. Johnston, E. Paltrige and Francis.

December 26th, Brethren Sawtell and Grove were appointed auditors.

An effort was made to devise ways and means to liquidate the debt upon the building by the 1st of May next. A committee consisting of Brethren Beardsall, Wolverton, Karn, Sawtell and Grove to attend to the matter.

It was moved that at the next annual meeting seven deacons be elected.

Annual meeting January 17th, 1883, Pastor Trotter occupied the chair.

The treasurer's report was read, but referred back to have it include a full report of the various branches of church work.

Reports from the assistant treasurer, cemetery, poor fund and Sabbath schools were read and adopted.

Bro. Grove accepted the leadership of the choir.

Bro. Catling superintendent of "Beneficent card plan."

The deacons now resigned when the church accepted each resignation and thanked them for faithful services.

The meeting then proceeded to elect by ballot, according to the new constitution, resulting in the choice of Brethren Pavey, Biggins, Karn, Hatch, Catling, Farmer and Beardsall. C. C. Carryer re-elected church clerk.

February 20th, Mrs. Farmer was appointed organist at a salary of $50 per annum.

It was resolved that the annual general meeting of the members as named in clause 4, article 3 in rules and regulations, shall be held on the 1st Friday in June 1884, and that the deacons elect be then set apart by the "laying on of hands."

April 9th, the following were appointed delegates to the "Baptist Union" to meet in Brantford the 30th inst., viz: Brethren Beardsall, Farmer, Hatch, Pavey, Sawtell and the pastor.

April 23rd, a verbal report was presented by the committee asking that the time for paying off the debt be extended to October 1st and the trustees to have charge of the matter.— adopted.

It was also decided to pay the pastor's salary monthly.

May 15th, installation services were held when a large number from Toronto and elsewhere attended the meeting.

May 21st, a large committee was appointed to provide for our first annual members' meeting in June.

Delegates from this church to the association in Port Rowan were appointed as follows: The Pastor, Karn, Catling, Beardsall, Biggins, Topping and Wolverton. Beardsall to write the circular letter.

The statistics showed a membership of 309, and amount raised for church and mission purposes $3,384. Number of S. S. scholars 174 —J. I. Bates, superintendent. East Mission 90 scholars—D. W. Karn, superintendent.

June 6th, today was inaugurated an annual members' meeting for social and spiritual converse and edification and praise, and never in the history of the church was there held so loving and delightful a meeting of its members as a family in the Lord's service. Beginning at 2 p. m. and holding a session of praise and speaking of God's goodness till 6 p. m., when till 8 p. m. tea was served. The evening session was similarly occupied with the addition of reading letters from absent members, A donation of $177 towards the debt was contributed. Such was the interest that the pastor failed to get the meeting closed till 11 p. m. All seemed delighted with this new departure.

Bro. Trotter, while attending McMaster Hall, had always arranged to be present at the ordinance, and up to the present had received new members every month by baptism or letter. He was therefore granted a much needed holiday.

October 26th, the deacons recommended that the scheme proposed to raise three cents per member per week for educational purposes be adopted.—Carried unanimously.

November 18th, the pastor introduced the subject of church socials, recommending holding them more frequently when a committee consisting of the pastor and Brethren Karn and Sawtell was appointed to arrange for the same.

The first was held the 28th and was well attended and profitable.

The union prayer meetings of 1885 produced good results and were continued every evening in our own church, so that the usual annual and monthly meetings were not held till February 19th, when the usual reports were presented and adopted.

A committee consisting of R. W. Sawtell, W. Biggins and D. W. Karn was appointed to take steps to erect a mission school house in the east end and report to the church.

March 1st, The pastor gave the hand of fellowship to 16 new members.

April 5th, the hand of fellowship was given to several members before the ordinance of the Lord's supper and after the evening service others were baptized.

On the 15th, Brethren Hoile, D. W. Karn, R. W. Sawtell, J. Beardsall and the Pastor were appointed delegates to the Baptist union and one dollar per each delegate to be sent to the union.

April 20th, the deacons reported the results of the revision of the church roll when a number of names were dropped therefrom for "non attendance and unheard from for years."

Instructions were given to make improvements in the porch of the church.

May 20th, Brethren Farmer, Beardsall, Wolverton, C. Schofield and the pastor were appointed to attend the association at Brownsville. Present membership 324; amount raised during the year $3,323; scholars in Sunday school 260; contributions $97; J. I. Bates superintendent.

The annual members meeting was held on the 5th of June when 188 were present and many responded by letter and contribution to the funds. A very social and profitable time was spent together.

July 15th, Brethren Farmer and Bates were delegated to sit in council on the ordination of Bro. Stillwell.

The east end mission committee were authorized to purchase a lot from Mrs. Frizelle.

September 14th, the question of erecting a new building for the east mission was discussed and referred back to the committee for further information as to cost.

September 23rd it was "resolved to engage an architect to prepare plans for the improvements to be made in the church," and a committee was appointed to solicit subscriptions for the east end mission house and for a new pipe organ. The present one having failed to give satisfaction.

October 28, R. W. Sawtell reported for the trustees that they deem it unwise to incur the expenses of an architect at present until some definite plans for raising the funds for enlargement are matured, and in their opinion a local architect should be engaged when necessary. The report was laid upon the table.

The pastor and deacon Beardsall were delegated to attend the ordination of Bro. Avauche at Stratford.

R. G. Sawtell presented the report of the committee for east mission which recommended a social to be held on the 17th of November. Report adopted.

November 18th, the mission school and pipe organ for the church were again discussed and a resolution passed asking the trustees to proceed at once with both objects.

November 25th, Mr. Trotter stated to the meeting that circumstances were such that he was under the necessity of severing his connection with the church, which he deeply regretted, because he loved the church as he never expected to love another, and his relations with the brethren were without a flaw. On being pressed for his reasons he admitted that he must have a larger salary to meet the obligations he was called upon to discharge, and feeling that the Woodstock church was paying as much as it ought, he had indicated to the Park church, Brantford, that he would accept the liberal offer made him by that church.

Mr. Trotter then left to allow the church to discuss the matter.

Deacon Pavey was appointed chairman and Bro. Wolverton moved a very lengthy resolution to the effect that the church could not allow his needs to stand in the way of his remaining the pastor of this church. That we thank him for his frank and manly statement and urge him to withdraw his resignation agreeing to increase his salary to more than the amount offered by the church referred to.

A committee was appointed to canvass for special contributions to make up the required amount, and Brethren Karn, Wolverton and R. H. Burtch to present the resolution passed and urge him to remain the pastor of this church.

December 2nd, Bro. Beardsall reported the result of the canvass as entirely satisfactory—more than the increase required had been subscribed.

December 9th, Mr. Trotter intimated that on the action taken by the church as expressed in the resolution of November 25th, and the report of the committee as given December 2nd he would withdraw his resignation.

December 16th, it was resolved that in consequence of unforseen circumstances, the committee defer the purchase of a new pipe organ for the present but that the one in the gallery be removed to the tower and a reed organ be used in its place.

The pastor was authorized to select a suitable hymn book for use in the prayer meetings.

January 27th, 1886, R. W. Sawtell reported from the trustees that work on the mission school on the lot purchased from Mr. Frizelle was progressing as fast as the weather permits.

One hundred copies of Sanky and Moody's hymn books were ordered.

The clerk was asked to retire when a resolution was passed, expressing the thanks of the church, and to be accompanied by a donation of $50 to C. C. Carryer, for so many years, faithful service.

The adjourned annual business meeting was held January 28th. The various usual reports were read and adopted.

A report from an informal meeting of deacons and trustees, held at the house of D. W. Karn, for the purpose of considering the propriety of providing increased seating accommodation in the audience-room, was read, recommending the outlay of $1,000 and giving additional seating room for 160 persons.

The report was adopted, and a committee consisting of Messrs. Karn, Sawtell, Biggins and R. H. Burtch to mature plans and report in two weeks.

Bro. Clifford resigned the office of sexton. At the close of the meeting, Pastor Trotter, in a few appropriate words of esteem and confidence from the church, presented Bro. Carryer with a check for the sum of $50, as instructed at a former meeting.

Bro. Carryer was quite overcome with the kindness expressed, and said that he felt stronger and better for such an expression.

February 10th—It was moved and seconded that the committee mature plans and secure tenders for the proposed enlargement, and that Bro. Sawtell be chairman of the building committee.

Sunday, March 7th, the hand of fellowship was given to ten new members.

The pastor asked the church to add another new deacon to the board, by election, at an early meeting.

Special meeting, March 10th, called to discuss the plans and specifications, when, after various suggestions, the report was adopted by 27 to 4 to proceed with the work at once.

Delegates to the Baptist Union at Toronto were appointed as follows: The pastor and Deacons Hatch, Karn, Pavey and Beardsall.

It was resolved to ask for the use of the town hall while the alterations were being made.

Bro. R. H. Burtch was duly elected deacon of the church.

Notwithstanding but four votes against the plans for enlargement, a feeling, subsequently obtained, that it would be wiser to enlarge the building for permanentcy, than to spoil it by galleries. Other meetings were held and larger plans and sketches made. A special meeting was called, May 12th, when a report was presented, and the plans adopted for a large extension to the west, and a re-arrangement of the entire audience-room, and completion of the spire, which never had been finished. The

G

estimates then submitted amounted to $6,620, but it subsequently became enlarged to nearly $11,000, including a new pipe organ, by Warren, of Toronto, at a cost of $1,550.

The trustees were authorized to mortgage the property for the sum required, and proceed forthwith. A measure of enthusiasm was thrown into the work that was a surprise to the whole church. Cuthbertson & Fowler were the architects, and Bickerton & Co., the contractors. D. W. Karn and R. W. Sawtell, inspectors, and the latter chairman of the building committee.

A large committee was appointed to arrange for the annual members' meeting in June. The donations were to go towards the extension, and determined to raise at least $2,000 for that object during the year.

Wednesday, May 26th—The pastor and R. W. Sawtell were appointed delegates to sit in council in Guelph on the 3rd of June, at the proposed ordination of Bro. W. C. Weir.

The members' annual meeting was held June 4th, when the attendance was large. A letter from J. McLaurin, who had returned a second time to India, together with many others from absent members, were read and greatly enjoyed. Many branches of church work were referred to, and a very delightful and profitable time was spent together. The pastor referred to the large number of deaths during the year—seven.

The Grand River association was held here on the 10th to 12th of June. The attendance was large, and the whole meeting was of an exceptionally pleasant character.

Rev. Mr. Ware preached the association sermon. The delegates from our own church were the pastor and Brethren Havens, Beardsall, Catling, Sawtell and Leadbeater. Total number of members reported, 330. Contributions for the year, $3,202. Number of scholars, 210; contributions, $140. J. I. Bates, supt. East school, No. 107, contributions, $67. Supt., Mr. Waldo.

June 16th, the pastor and Deacons Pavey and Beardsall were delegated to attend a council at Goble's to ordain Brother Frazer June 22. The pastor and Deacons Hatch and Beardsall to attend a council at Springford on the 28th June, to ordain Bro. McLennan.

June 26th, 1886—The death of our beloved brother, Rev. W. H. Landon, is recorded. His activity and zeal for souls began with his membership, in the very earliest days of the church's history, and except for the few years spent in the West Indies, and a few other years when he isolated himself, on account of difference of views, his labors were abundant and freely given, " without money and without price."

A short time before he died a very pleasant surprise party, headed by the pastor, took possession of his house and cheered his declining days, by an appreciative address and a present. He expressed his extreme pleasure with the unexpected event, and said it would be a sweet memoir of the continued love of the church, to which he was so deeply attached.

He left a widow who is still an active and beloved member of the church.

July 19th, the pastor was voted a vacation.

September 30th, a joint meeting of the church and college was held in the latter place this evening, for the purpose of designating and bidding farewell to our beloved sister, Miss Bella Hatch, who was intending to devote her life and energies to zenanna work among the Telugus of India.

October 6th, the pastor and Brethren Bates, Beardsall, Wolverton, Karn, Burtch and Pavey were appointed delegates to the convention to be held at Paris. The "Baptist Union" had not succeeded in its object, and the denomination returned to the usual fall convention with some changes in its constitution.

November 24th—It was decided by the church to organize an association to be called "The Women's Committee for Church Work," to meet monthly, or oftener, to discuss and take up the required work of the church—rightly considered their special work.

An application was sent to the church from Ionia, Mich., asking it to send a delegate to the ordination of Bro. T. S. McCall

On Sabbath December 19th, 1886, after worshipping in the

town hall for six months the church returned to its enlarged and beautiful home.

Rev. Dr. Thomas, of Toronto, preached in the forenoon. Rev. W. Cuthbertson, Congregational minister at Woodstock in the afternoon and Dr. Thomas in the evening. Nearly 1,000 people attended each service. Prof. E. R. Doward, organist of Jarvis street church, Toronto, presided at the splendid new organ and with a good choir produced excellent music.

It is not necessary to describe the handsome and commodious building which was this day reopened. Its appearance and accoustics are all that could be wished for and its conveniences for Sabbath school and general purpose excellent. As before stated the cost including new carpets, upholstering and organ amounted to nearly $11,000, but in every respect it is equal to an entirely new building and strangers have no conception from the interior but that it was all planned from the beginning.

Church meeting December 22nd. W. H. Whitehead was appointed sexton, J. Hoyle having resigned. The resignation of Bro.Topping as trustee was accepted and a vote of thanks given him for long services.

December 29th, W. Biggins was elected trustee.

The North part of the church was set apart for the accommodation of the lady students and the south gallery to gentlemen.

Several changes have taken place in the College during the last year. A charter had been obtained establishing "McMaster University by act of parliament to include Woodstock College, McMaster Hall, Toronto, to which the theological department had been removed from Woodstock some years ago, and an arts department which it was intended and expected to be established in Woodstock. Mr. Wolverton had resigned the position of principal here which he had so faithfully occupied since the death of Principal Torrance and D. Rand had been induced to take his place on the understanding that the arts department should be developed here ; hence on Sunday morning, January 2nd, Dr. T. H. Rand and wife were admitted members of this church by letter from Toronto.

Large numbers of new candidates were applying for baptism Bro. Ware was assisting the pastor in evening meetings so that the January business meeting usually held was omitted.

Feb. 17th, the annual business meeting was held and the usual reports adopted.

It was, according to previous notice "resolved to close our associational year on the 15th of May and the annual business meeting be held on the last Wednesday in May.

March 6, 1887, at the business meeting this evening the pastor stated that he needed a long vacation and with the permission of the church he wanted to visit his native land, England, and would be absent 4 months. He felt sure that as the deacons could secure the services of Bro. H. C. Spellar for the whole period the church would the more readily grant his request.

A resolution referring to the late severe work of the pastor in the ingathering of such a large number of new members and his great need of a vacation, the request was concurred in and kind expressions for his welfare and safe return were embodied in the resolution unanimously passed by a standing vote.

Almost every week candidates were examined and received for baptism and the hand of fellowship given on the first Sabbath of each month.

Wednesday April 20th, the lecture room was filled and the usual business gave place to a delightful meeting presided over by the pastor, who after giving his own farewell address introduced Bro. Spellar as the substitute during his absence. Bro. Spellar made a very practical and humorous address. Kind expressions were given to Mr. Trotter in his voyage and prospective future.

April 27th, Bro. King was granted a license to preach the gospel.

May 1st, the hand of fellowship was given by Pastor Spellar to 10 new members.

May 16th, Messrs. Spellar, Farmer, Pavey, Wolverton, R. H. Burtch and R. W. Sawtell were appointed delegates to the as-

sociation to be held at Beachville. Number of members 399.
Amount expended $13,671.

June 3rd the members' meeting was held as usual and proved
quite as interesting as previous ones. In addition to exercises
of a devotional and social character the secretary of the trustees
gave a full report of the finances of the church, showing that
$7,099.04 had been raised in cash during the year.

. June 28th, a public meeting was held this evening for the
purpose of giving expressions of welcome to Bro. McLaurin and
wife whose return from India to save his life, if not to restore
his health, was their reason for returning. So low was he with
fever that he was reported dead and Mrs. McLaurin never expected to bring him home alive, but the sea voyage had so help-
ed him as to enable him to be present on this occasion and re
ceive the spontaneous welcome accorded. Rev. Mr. Woodward
represented the Grand River association. The Rev. Mr. Cuthbertson the ministers of the town. Mr.T.S.Shenston the Foreign
Missionary Society. Pastor Spellar presided and gave the
address of ~'elcome to his own church and Rev. Bro. McLaurin
replied in feeble voice but loving and wise words.

The hand of fellowship was given to 9 new members July 3rd.

July 20th, Bro. W. Johnston was appointed superintendent
of the East Sabbath school.

Bro. Walter Watts reported that it was the intention of the
Young People's association to purchase a piano for the Sabbath
school and asked the church to hold a lawn social on that behalf
—granted.

A letter was read from Rev.E.Judson thanking the church for
a donation towards the Judson memorial church erected in New
York

September 9th,1887,a meeting was held to welcome home Pastor Trotter and wife from their visit to the Old Land. Mr.
Spellar occupied the chair. R. W. Sawtell read the address
from the church, Dr. Rand spoke on behalf of the college and
Mr. Wolverton the Sabbath school. Rev. Dr. Castle, Rev. Mr.

Turnbull and Rev. Mr. Landon each added their expressions of welcome.

Bro. Trotter feelingly replied on the part of himself and wife—formerly Miss Freeman.

September 28th, the delegates appointed to the convention in Toronto were the Pastor, Dr. Rand, Rev's J. McLaurin and Wolverton, D. W. Karn, R. W. Sawtell and J. H. Farmer.

The pastor and Dr. Rand were appointed to sit in council at Toronto October 9th, to ordain Bro. Garside, missionary elect for India and formerly a student here.

October 26th, on motion of Dr. Rand a resolution was passed to invite the Home Mission Society through the board of governors of the University to meet in Woodstock in April or May of next year to hold an educational meeting in reference to the arts department

December 7th Bro. Grove resigned the leadership of the choir, which was accepted, and a resolution passed expressing the thanks of the church for his long and faithful services. Mr. E. M. Karn was appointed to the position of leader.

The anniversary of the reopening of the church was held on the 19th December when Rev. Dr. Denovan preached morning and evening to a very full house.

On Monday evening Dr. Denovan delivered a lecture on "The Great Revival in Ireland," which was intensely interesting. Miss Grove presided at the organ and some choice vocal solos were given by Mr. and Mrs. G McLeod. The pastor gave a statement of the financial position of the church and asked that $400 be made up during the meetings. A sum amounted to $411 was announced as the result of both day's collections.

March 14, 1888, a special meeting of the church was called to elect delegates to attend the educational meeting to be held at Guelph, to decide the questions discussed in Toronto at the autumn convention but not then decided, First: Independence versus confederation with the Provincial University," second, locating the arts department of McMaster University.

Having referred to the object of this meeting it becomes

necessary to make a brief explanation. Several years ago a
similar meeting was held in Guelph also, to discuss the removal
of the theological department from Woodstock to Toronto. The
attendance of delegates was large and the discussion at times
warm; and the vote if taken would have been largely in favor
of remaining in Woodstock, but at the point of deciding Dr.
Castle, then in the confidence of Mr. McMaster, made a
statement to the effect that if taken to Toronto the necessary
buildings would be provided and probably an endowment, but
he was not at liberty to say more. It was evident that the
matter could be left in such hands. It was well known that
Mr. McMaster had set his heart upon the work and it was at
once decided to let him. The result was that McMaster hall
(subsequently named against his wish) was erected at a cost of
about $80,000 and largely endowed, and the theological depart-
ment removed thereto—leaving the literary department doing
the first year's university work—and the ladies department still
at Woodstock.

In 1880 and '81 a canvas for an endowment of $50,000 and
for $10,000 to pay the debt at Woodstock had been made by
Mr. Dyke to which it was liberally subscribed and a large part
of the subscriptions paid.

Subsequently, the subscribers of the old C. L. Institute, at
the Paris convention, agreed to surrender their rights and management to the denomination, "provided it should be consoli-
dated and developed."

Later on a charter was obtained from the Ontario Government constituting McMaster University, when it was understood
that the arts department would be developed at Woodstock.
"The first of a series of buildings" was erected for a dining hall
(and a second one planned) looking to the future requirements
of the university, costing nearly $30,000, and the foundation
stone of which was laid by Mrs. McMaster, in the presence of
a large assembly, including the Hon. Mr.McMaster. The people
of Woodstock had been solicited for subscriptions to the amount
of $10,000 towards the erection of buildings for the art depart-

ment, and had pledged $11,000 for that purpose, in anticipation of this becoming a university town.

Expectation ran high, and when it was learned in the summer of 1887 that the location of the arts department was unsettled, and that the question would be reopened and fully discussed in Toronto at the October convention, the friends of Woodstock college, and particularly the people of Woodstock, were astounded, and could not believe the rumor. Mr. McMaster died suddenly before the discussion was opened.

Previous to the October meeting in Toronto the Baptist opened its columns for a full discussion, and it was hotly argued as " Woodstock vs. Toronto." At the meeting held in Toronto, the question of " Independency" was discussed, and, virtually, decided to oppose confederation, but the vote was reserved for a special meeting, to be held at Guelph, on the 27th of March, 1888.

The delegates named from our own church were : The pastor, Dr. Rand, R. W. Sawtell, D. W. Karn, N. Wolverton, J. H. Farmer and J. I. Bates, who were elected by ballot.

The town subscribers elected Messrs. John White, J. M. Grant and J. Sutherland, M. P., to represent their interests at the meeting.

The meeting was held in the Baptist church, Guelph, and upwards of 500 delegates were present. The question of " Independency vs. Confederation," excited but little interest, and the vote was almost unanimous in favor of the former.

The exciting question was the location ; but those favorable to Toronto had organized their forces to better advantage, and, by introducing a plausible clause in their resolution to respect the " moral obligation to Woodstock," and other well ordered plans, secured a small majority in favor of Toronto. It is needless to add that the friends of Woodstock college were not only surprised but dissatisfied, and the town subscribers held an indignation meeting to condemn the whole arrangement.

The church here felt humiliated and disgraced by the breaking of faith with the Woodstock subscribers, and all who had been led to believe that "Mr. McMaster had acquiesed in the purpose of developing the arts work here, and had made his will with that in view." The church openly expressed its disapproval in a meeting held to hear the report of the delegates.

The occurrence is so recent and so well understood that a fuller statement seems unneccessary; but in justice to the Woodstock church the reference now made could not be avoided.

The following delegates were elected, March 21st, to attend a council at London South, to recognize a new church there, viz.: Brethren Beardsall, Catling, Pavey, McLaurin, Bates and the pastor.

April 1st, a number of new members were admitted to the communion by the hand of fellowship.

B. W. A. Grigg was duly licensed to preach.

May 6th, a number of new members were added.

May 16th, Miss Grove's resignation as organist was formally accepted, and a resolution of thanks and regret that circumstances caused her to leave town, was passed—her parents having removed to Galt.

Brother McLaurin asked the privilege of arranging for a lecture from Miss Reynolds, the lady principal of the college, in aid of the "Timpany Memorial." Granted.

June 5th, Brethren Beardsall, Hatch, Wolverton, Bates, Farmer and Favey were appointed delegates to the association at Springford. Brother Farmer to write the letter.

May 28th, the annual business meeting was held, when all the usual reports were read and received.

It was resolved, "That it would facilitate the business to dispense with the assistant treasurer, and that Brother Beardsall be asked to hold the position occupied next year."

June 1st, it was reported that Pastor Trotter was too ill to attend. Brother Farmer was elected chairman of the members' meeting.

About 200 members were present. Afternoon and evening sessions were held, and tea served between. The reports which had been received at the business meeting were read, discussed and adopted.

Brother Beardsall accepted the office of treasurer, in place of D. W. Karn, resigned.

W. Chave was appointed superintendent of the card plan. N. Wolverton resigned the superintendency of the Central Sabbath school, and D. W. Karn succeeded him.

A resolution, expressive of condolence, sympathy and love for the pastor in his affliction, was passed, and a promise made to supply the pulpit during the continuance of his sickness.

Mr. E. M. Karn was appointed leader of the choir and organist, for one year, at a salary of $150.

The statistics sent to the association were: Members, 401 ; contributions, $6,189 ; S. S. scholars, 256.

August 5th—In the continued absence of Brother Trotter, the pulpit to-day was supplied by Rev. S. S. Bates, who administered the ordinance of the Lord's Supper. The hand of fellowship was given to several members by Brother McLaurin.

August 15th J. McLaurin occupied the chair. After the disposal of several reports, Deacon Beardsall read the resignation of Brother Trotter, whose illness compelled him to take the step.

It was decided not to accept the resignation then, but call a special meeting in two weeks for the purpose of considering it.

August 22nd on motion of J. Beardsall a license was granted to Bro. Catling to preach the gospel.

September 2nd Brother Wolverton preached and gave the hand of fellowship to a number of new members.

September 19th—Regular monthly meeting. Brother Wolverton in the chair.

Delegates appointed to the convention at St. Catharines were : Brethren Wolverton, McKechnie, Sawtell, McLaurin, Hatch, Beardsall and Karn.

It was moved by Brother Sawtell, seconded by Brother Potts, "That the resignation of Pastor Trotter be accepted, and that Brother Wolverton notify him in a letter expressive of the sympathy of the church.

A resolution was passed instructing the deacons to take the necessary steps to procure a pastor.

October 16th—Brother McLaurin in the chair. A license was granted Brother J. Roberts to preach, and the chairman to sign the same.

October 18th the deacons brought in a report favoring a call to the Rev. E. W. Dadson, of Claremont, to the pastorate of this church.

The adoption of the report was moved by Brother Wolverton, seconded by Brother Karn and carried by a standing vote.

A committee was appointed to confer with Brother Dadson in reference to the " call."

A request was presented from the "Ladies' Circle," asking the church to co-operate with them in inviting the Ladies' Missionary Convention to meet at Woodstock next year. Request concurred in—with the promise to assist, also, in the entertainment of delegates.

October 31st it was resolved to hold the anniversary services about the 19th of December. A committee was appointed, with J. H. Farmer chairman. Brethren Gould and Duncan were appointed ushers in place of Brethren Johnston and Catling, who had left town.

November 21st Brother A. Havens was elected trustee in place of E. H. Grove, removed.

It was announced that a telegram had been received from Brother Dadson, accepting the call of the church to the pastorate.

Brother Topping appealed to the church, on a ruling of Chairman Beardsall at a former meeting, in reference to an old matter decided ten years ago. The chairman was sustained by a large vote.

December 2nd, 1888, Pastor Dadson occupied the pulpit and preached from Acts 2 ch., 47 v. He gave the hand of fellowship to several members before the ordinance, including Rev. S. S. Sheldon, teacher at the college.

December 16th Brother Dadson preached sermons appropriate to the anniversary of re-opening. On Monday evening Rev.

A. H. Munro, of St. Thomas, lectured. Collections were taken each day in favor of the building fund.

December 19th the report of the supply committee was adopted and the committee discharged. Deacons' report read and partially adopted. It was resolved to take a collection January 6th, to aid the widow of the late Rev. H. Woodward.

January 6th, 1889, Rev. N. Wolverton gave the hand of fellowship to Mr. and Mrs. Dadson and others.

January 16th—Regular monthly meeting. A number of candidates were received for baptism and letters of dismission granted.

January 23rd Brother J. McLaurin spoke on the great needs of the foreign mission, urging the church to support one missionary there.

Sunday, January 27th, several were baptized.

March 30th several were received by letter, and some dismissed, also by letter.

A committee, consisting of the pastor, Prof. Farmer and Bro. McAlpine, were appointed to take charge of the east end mission and report to the church.

April 7th the pastor gave the hand of fellowship to ten new members, and in the evening baptized several others.

April 16th the pastor and Deacon Beardsall were appointed to attend the ordination council at Plattsville, to ordain Mr. T. Shields.

May 5th, the pastor gave the hand of fellowship to thirteen new members.

May 15th, the " Woodstock Association " to be held at Beachville this year, and the following be delegates from this church, viz.: The pastor, J. Beardsall, W. Pavey, J. H. Farmer, R. W. Sawtell, A. L. Haven and C. Duncan. N. Wolverton to write the circular letter.

May 19th —Baptism this evening.

Letters to the association read and approved.

Statistics showing total number of members, after dropping 24, whose present standing was unknown, or had neglected their church privilege, was 394. Total amount paid for all objects, $5,075. S. S. scholars, 281; teachers, 36. Amount received, $171.

Mission school: Number of scholars, 120 ; teachers, 20. Amount raised, $144.

May 26th, the pastor baptized five candidates.

Annual business meeting was held May 31st, when all the usual reports were read and adopted, a vote was passed, expressing thanks to Brother Beardsall for his faithful work as treasurer.

A very cordial vote of thanks was tendered to Grandma Burtch for her successful efforts in collecting special subscriptions of over $200, to apply to the reduction of the debt.

Brother Beardsall was re-elected treasurer, and Brother Carryer clerk. Brethren A. L. Havens and N. McKechnie were elected deacons by ballot.

Sunday, June 2nd, the hand of fellowship was extended to eleven new members, and others baptized in the evening of the same day.

The members' annual meeting was held June 7th. Pastor Dadson conducted the afternoon and evening meetings, which were more deeply interesting than ever. According to previous notice, the three deacons recently elected were ordained by the " laying on of hands."

Two hundred and twenty members took tea together and enjoyed a social time.

June 16th, letters of brotherly greeting were read from Brother T. Trotter, from Nova Scotia, and Brother J. I. Bates, then pursuing his studies in Manchester, England.

Several were baptized in the evening.

June 19th, Brother McAlpine reported that it was advisable to appoint Brother Kennedy to the charge of the east mission, and the church approved of the same.

June 22nd, the hand of fellowship was given to four members, and on July 7th to nineteen more, and others baptized the same evening, and others on the 14th.

Business meeting July 17th, pastor in the chair, A.L. Havens acting as clerk.

Deacons' monthly report read and adopted.

The motion of Brother McLaurin, "That the question of missions be discussed the first Wednesday in September," was adopted.

August 21st, it was decided to grant the use of the church for a farewell meeting to our missionaries, on the 5th of September, and a committee appointed to make arrangements for the same.

Sabbath, September 1st, eight members received the hand of fellowship.

September 4th, a public meeting was held to listen to Brethren Walker and Brown, and say farewell on the eve of their leaving as missionaries to the Telugus. The meeting was large and inspiring.

Monthly meeting September 15th. Several new members were received by letter, and others dismissed the same way.

Deacons' report read and approved.

Brother D. Nimmo, having been heard by the church, was granted a license to preach.

The delegates appointed to attend the convention at Ottawa, in October, were: the pastor, and Brethren T. P. Hall, R. W. Sawtell, J. McLaurin, C. Hatch, R. H. Burtch and J. Beardsall.

October 2nd—Having learned that the church only allowed our present membership to send five delegates, it was resolved, "That the first five elected be the delegation."

A resolution was passed, moved by N. S. McKechnie, seconded by D Clark, "that we tend an invitation to the convention now assembling, to meet with us next year."

Brother W. H. Huston and wife were received as members, on their letters to this church.

In reference to the work of the convention held at Ottawa, it might be stated that it was a very large and enthusiastic one, especially in regard to missions and French evangelization.

Another important movement was the enthusiastic adoption, of Brother D. S. Thompson's resolution, condemning the prin-

ciple of "exemption from taxation of church property and ministers' incomes."

Considerable dissatisfaction was expressed in regard to the
removal of the ladies' department from Woodstock to Toronto,
which had been the work chiefly of Dr. McVicar, the chancellor
of McMaster University who had influenced Mrs. McMaster to
assist in founding Moulton's Ladies College instead.

The matter of beginning the arts work in McMaster Hall was
discussed and largely disapproved, but not brought to a vote.

Professor Farmer had been principal of Woodstock College
since the retirement of Dr. Rand, but being elected to a chair
in Toronto Baptist College, Bro. W. H. Huston, principal of
one of the Collegiate Colleges of Toronto was appointed to take
his place. Brother Wolverton had succeeded in inducing the
governors to establish a manner training department—the first
in Canada—at the Woodstock College and as head of that department had made it a great success. In response to the
"moral obligation clause" Chancellor McVicar had succeeded
in making very large changes in the building and equipment
here and, with the first year's University work continued, Bro.
Huston had accepted the charge of Principal with great enthu-
siam and threw all his energy and love into the work of training his "boys."

"The Women's Baptist Misssionary Convention" was held in
this church October 24th and 25th, when a very large number
of delegates attended. The meetings were open to the public,
and a large number availed themselves of the opportunity of
seeing women transact business ; and many were honest enough
to confess that in prompt, business management, and short,
effective speaking, they put to shame some of the more preten-
tious efforts of the "stronger" sex.

At the close of the second afternoon session, the convention
accepted the invitation of Principal Huston and his faculty to
a reception at the college, and a delightful evening was spent
there, taxing largely the space and hospitalities of that large
institution ; but leaving pleasant memories of Woodstock and

the entertainment given during the whole of the convention. The Woodstock church will cherish as a fragrant blessing the coming to it of so many inspiring friends, and a longing for a repetition of such.

October 27th the pastor and Brethren Topping and Beardsall were delegated to sit in council at Clinton, in regard to some church difficulty.

Sabbath, November 3rd, the hand of fellowship was extended by the pastor to eight members, including Brethren Huston and Robertson, teachers at the college.

November 6th it was decided, on motion of Brother Wolverton, that "thanksgiving services be held this year at the college."

November 20th Brother McAlpin made a verbal report, showing the necessity of enlarging the mission school premises.

After a full discussion, the pastor and Brethren Wolverton, McLaurin, Sawtell and Burtch, were appointed a committee to investigate the matter and report to the church.

The deacons recommended an increase of $200 per annum in the pastor's salary—carried by a standing vote.

The deacons' report was taken up seriatim and discussed. The Sabbath school was granted the use of the audience room for their entertainment.

The pastor reported on behalf of the hymn book committee, advising the adoption of the new edition of the Sankey and Moody hymns.

December 4th Brother Wolverton, chairman of the committee on missions, reported, recommending (1), the strengthening of the east end mission—carried ; (2), on repairs and enlargement —laid upon the table ; (3), that the matter of building there and the west end be referred to the trustees for a report thereon.

December 18th on motion of N. Wolverton, seconded by W. Pavey, it was "resolved, That this church do proceed to establish a mission interest in the west end of the town."

A committee consisting of the trustees and others was appointed to proceed, with power to purchase a site for the same.

H

January 5th, 1890, the hand of fellowship was extended to several new members.

January 15—Monthly business meeting. A number were received by letter and for baptism.

Brother Dadson announced that special evangelistic meetings would be held, beginning on Monday evening. During the whole year of 1889 there had been a continual ingathering. No month had passed without a considerable increase ; and now there were indications (after the week of prayer) of a deep interest in spiritual things and he desired to give greater opportunity for its manifestation.

February 17th after the prayer meeting the regular business was transacted, Deacons' rep.rt read and adopted.

On motion of Bro. Biggins a committee was appointed to arrange an after tea social on the 28th inst.

Dr. McLay and Principal Huston were appointed to look after unruly boys who are in the habit of disturbing the East Mission.

Reports were made in reference to sites obtainable in the west end and other matters, when the committee was requested to bring in a report upon "ways and means."

February 26th, R. G. Sawtell, assistant superintendant of the Central Sunday school, asked the church to supply the school with the new hymn book such as is now used in the prayer meeting—request granted.

Brother Wolverton, chairman, reported that the committee had purchased two lots, with a frame dwelling on one of them, on the corner of Oxford and Hunter streets, for the sum of $1,-400, and the deed would be made to R. W. Sawtell to hold till the trustees were prepared to accept it and assume the responsibility and the liability on the same.

March 2nd, the Pastor extended the hand of fellowship to 9 members.

Sabbath April 6th, the hand of fellowship was extended by the Pastor to 11 new members.

April 16th, business meeting, Deacons' report received and adopted.

Brethren Topping and Pavey were appointed to draft a letter of appreciation of the services of Brother Carryer on his retiring from his duties after so many years of faithful services as church clerk.

Brother D. K. Clarke was appointed clerk and he with brethren Carryer and Pavey were appointed to assist the Judson mission society of the College to obtain historical information asked for by said society.

May 21st, Brother Wolverton reported the progress made in reference to the new building and subscriptions for the west end when a committee was appointed to collect the subscriptions as they become due and pay the same to the treasurer of the trustees, R. W. Sawtell.

The delegates appointed to attend the association to be held at Scotland this year were Brethren Hatch, Duncan, Bates, Beardsall, R. G. Sawtell, McLaurin, Miss Hatch and the Pastor. Total number of members 450.

A resolution moved by Brother Topping condemning the sale and delivery of milk on the Sabbath and urging all Christians to fully observe the Sabbath as a day of rest and religious duties was carried.

May 28th, It was moved by N. Wolverton, seconded by R. W. Sawtell that the friends of the East Mission raise $50 by subscriptions towards paying a student for the summer.

May 30th, yearly financial meeting. The reports from every department of church work were read, received and laid over for discussion and adoption at the members' meeting.

The following officers were then appointed: Treasurer, J. Beardsall ; clerk, D. K. Clarke ; treasurer of the building fund, R. W. Sawtell ; Poor Fund, Deacon Pavey ; benevolent scheme, W. F. Chave ; superintendent of Central Sunday school, R. G. Sawtell ; east end, Bro. McAlpin.

Sabbath June 1st, the hand of fellowship was given to 12 new members.

The annual members meeting was very enthusiastically attended and a profitable time spent in the usual manner.

June 25th, Brethren McKechnie and D. K. Clarke were appointed to engage a student to supply the east mission pulpit. The $50 referred to having been subscribed.

June 29th, Brethren McLaurin and Beardsall were delegated to sit in council at Parliament street church, Toronto, to ordain a missionary elect for India.

July 16th, Deacon's report read and discussed seriatim and adopted.

The Pastor stated that the committee had elected Brother W. Winter to fill the pulpit at the east end, and having preached but once was taken down with fever and would probably die.

On motion of J. Beardsall, Brother McAlpin was appointed at the same salary to take up the work.

Brother Huston gave notice that in two months he would introduce a resolution in reference to the question of tax exemptions.

Brother Biggins asked to have his name withdrawn from the building committee, F. B. Scofield and W. Coventry were added.

September 10th, several committees were appointed to provide for the holding of the convention here in October.

Brethren Dadson, McLaurin, Sawtell, Chave, Wolverton, Huston and Whitelaw were appointed delegates to the same.

R. W. Sawtell reported that the west end church could be made ready for opening at the time of holding the convention and recommended that it be considered—referred to the building committee.

October 1st, the following resolutions were passed : (1) That Brother Wolverton be asked to preach the opening sermon at the west end, Oct. 19th. (2) Rev. S. S. Bates to preach in the afternoon and (3) Brother T. Trotter in the evening. (4) That Brother W. Coventry be appointed leader of the singing. (5) That the committee be instructed to procure a furnace for heating the building.

Brother McLaurin made request from Rural Dean Wade for the use of the audience room in which to hold a meeting in the interest of the "China Inland Mission" —request granted.

October 14th, the Deacons' report adopted.

A committee was appointed to take charge of socials.

The convention was held in the audience room and was very largely attended by delegates. The business as usual was crowded into too little time, but there was no very special or exciting subject discussed. The reports showed a very prosperous year's operations.

The new church was opened according to announcement and was well attended.

Nearly all the pulpits in town were supplied by delegates to the convention.

October 29th, letters of dismission were granted to 52 members to organize a new church at the west end to be called the "Oxford Street Baptist Church." Among the number were the two strongest advocates of the enterprize, viz: Brethren Wolverton and McLaurin. They have always felt that it was wrong to give up the west end school, and for some time agitated resuming and trying to recover the lost opportunity this time by starting a church for the convenience of our west end members. By persistent pleading Brother Wolverton at length got the members interested and the result has been the erection of a building capable of seating 300 persons costing about $2,-500, and the organizing of a church to which the "First Church" has dismissed about 80 of its members. The new church invited Rev. W. H. Tapscott to become its pastor, who accepted the position. A farewell social was held in the parent church to give expression to the good wishes of those who remained to those who formed the new church. Much credit is due to many earnest workers and contributors, but it would be invidious to mention any but Brother Wolverton, now principal of Bishop's College, Marshall, Texas, and Brother McLaurin who returned to his beloved work in India.

November 10th, a resolution was passed naming this church "The First Baptist Church."

Deacon Beardsall tendered his resignation of the treasurership having accepted the position of canvasser for the Grande Ligne Mission.

December 17, the Pastor and R. W. Sawtell were appointed to sit in council at Oxford Street church on the 29th inst., to recognize said church.

The question of publishing the contributions of all members to the various funds of the church was discussed and the resolution laid upon the table for one month.

Brethren Karn and R. W. Sawtell were appointed a committee to complete arrangements for the concert to be held on 22nd December. The proceeds to be devoted to the choir fund.

The Rev. T. S. Johnston, of London, to preach the anniversary sermons on the 21st

January 21st, 1891, the Deacon's report was read and adopted.

The discussion on the publication of names and contributions was resumed and adjourned after an informal vote largely in favor of the principal.

February 18th, the deacons report read and discussed clause by clause. In reference to one on the music question, a committee consisting of Brethren Karn, Huston, Mayberry, Bates and Sawtell was appointed to investigate and report at next meeting.

February 25th, the question of publication before referred to was finally voted on and carried in the affirmative—to come into effect with the present year.

The music committee reported in favor of proceeding (1) To secure new members for the choir. (2) To raise funds for the payment of necessary expenses and report quarterly to the church the condition of the choir.

March 18. Deacons' report read, discussed and finally adopted.

Brethren Feagles, Mitchell and Leadbeater were appointed ushers.

March 25th, the Pastor and Brethren C. S. Kerr and J. I. Bates were appointed a committee to suggest arrangements for supplying the Tuesday evening preaching for the summer months at the East Mission.

Wednesday, April 8th, the music committee reported that they were prepared to go on and engage the leader, Mr. Sturgis, and the soprano, Miss McDowell, if a guarantee fund of $200 were subscribed. The balance was then made up and the church affirmed the course proposed by the committee.

The east end committee reported that they had received promises from about twenty persons, willing to take charge of the services at the mission. The report was adopted and the committee continued.

April 15th, the deacons' report referred : (1) to revising the church roll; (2) the annual report of the various treasurers; (3) the annual letter, calling the members meeting; and (4) the church letter to the association—adopted.

Messrs. Mayberry and Chave were appointed auditors. A. O. McKee, treasurer, presented his quarterly report.

April 29th. A month's rest from preaching was voted to the pastor, on account of his suffering from sore throat.

May 20th. Deacon's report read and adopted. Delegates to the association : Brethren Beardsall, Surby, C. Duncan, R. G. Sawtell, J. I. Bates, A. Dickson, N. S. McKechnie, and the pastor.

May 22. The annual church meeting was held, and the usual routine business transacted. A vote of thanks was tendered to all the treasurers for efficient work done. The clerk and assistant treasurers were asked to co-operate with the treasurer in preparing the annual year-book.

Friday, June 5th, 1891, the annual members' meeting was held, the following report of which is copied from the "Sentinel-Review" of June 6th:

"The annual members' meeting of the First Baptist Church of this town has become an unalloyed pleasure to all who attend it; and the one that was held Friday last was equal, in every respect, to any former meeting. The object is of a social and edifying character; giving the members an opportunity to converse with each other, on their personal struggles and enjoyments in their christian life, and marking their growth in grace from year to year. The evening was particularly interesting in the fact : that during the past year this church erected a new place of worship in the west end of the town, and discharged by letter 52 of its members, who formed a new church, and now have a settled pastor. An invitation was extended to the new church members, and a large number availed themselves of the reunion. The pastor, Mr. Dadson, took the chair at 4 p.m., and an hour or two were pleasantly spent in prayer, praise, and speaking, one to another, of the goodness of God.

" Tea was served in the lecture-room from four to eight p.m., when the pastor resumed the chair, and, as in the afternoon, a large number of old and young spoke of the past and present. Probably the most inspiring talk was that from 'Grandma Burtch,' now about 87 years of age, and who has been a zealous member of the church over 65 years. She was grateful for being able to be present, which she had not expected. Another most interesting part of the programme, was the reading of letters from absent members, from India and other distant lands, as well as from various parts of this continent, nearly all of whom sent contributions towards the building fund—to which the thank-offering is devoted."

June 7th. New members were given the hand of fellowship before the ordinance, and in the evening others were baptised.

June 9th. At the request of the Ingersoll church, for delegates to meet in council there, to try and settle a difficulty which had arisen over some doctrinal point, the following were appointed, viz: Brethren Dadson, R. H. Burtch, and R. W. Sawtell.

September 16th. The deacons' report recommended the taking up a special collection to supplement contributions to home and foreign missions—adopted. The delegates appointed to the convention at Toronto were : the pastor, W. H. Huston, R. W. Sawtell, J. Beardsall, D. W. Karn. and J. Powell.

Brother Bates, for the committee of the east mission work, reported that it had been efficiently discharged during the summer. Report received and committee discharged.

Brother R. W. Sawtell was appointed to write the history of this church.

The brethren of Medicine Hat asked for a contribution—granted.

October 25th. The deacon's report received and read. It referred to the resignation of Miss Grove, organist; the anniversary services; social entertainments; Doe Lake church. Report adopted.

The music committee reported that Miss Ketchum was the only applicant for the position of organist, and had been engaged.

Brother Huston moved that the report of the music committee be confirmed; but, as this involved the question of authority of appointments, the matter was laid over for further consideration.

On the 20th of November, a public meeting was held in the First Baptist Church to say farewell to Brother McLaurin and family. It was largely attended by friends representing the denominational interests. Brother McLaurin had been here some years recruiting his health, and during part of the time was engaged as Foreign Mission Secretary, travelling from church to church all over the land and by his presence inspiring the denomination with the mission spirit. Now he felt his strength renewed, and he knew also, that some of the active workers disapproved of the system under which he was working. He resigned and accepted a position under the American Board in Bangalore, India, where the climate is favorable to his state of health. Expressions of deep sorrow were made at the convention in Toronto, but he could not be changed in his purpose. At this farewell meeting; very affecting addresses were made and replies given quite as effective. A beautiful portrait of brother McLaurin, painted by Brother C. Hatch, was unveiled and now hangs in the College chapel. Thus, for the third time our dear brother left his church, home and gave himself to the Foreign Mission work in India. A portrait of Mrs. McLaurin and youngest child was also painted by Mr. Hatch and sent after them to India as a present from her friends here.

November 18th, the deacons' report referred to seating of
students, appointing more ushers and the holding of special
services, all of which were dealt with.

Brother R. G. Sawtell was appointed to see that notices of
our church services are put in town papers.

Brethren Downs and Tegart were added to the staff of
ushers.

R. W. Sawtell reported the action of the committee on socials
and entertainments (1) A public reading in the town hall under
the auspices of the Young People's Society. (2) The anniversary sermons to be preached by Rev. Ira Smith of London, on
20th of December. (3) A sacred concert by the choir, under
the leadership of Mr. Sturgis on Monday evening, December
21st. (4) New Year's eve. suggested as a fitting time for the
S. S. cantata.—Report was adopted.

Sabbath, November 20th, candidates were baptized in the
evening.

December 16th, several candidates received for baptism.
Deacon Karn reported that the choir could not give the concert
proposed and it was decided to hold a social on the 21st, the
proceeds of which to be given to the choir fund.

Sabbath, January 3rd, 1892, the hand of fellowship was extended to 12 new members.

January 13th, R. W. Sawtell reported on the part of
the music committee that in consequence of circumstances
preventing the concert intended to be given by the choir
according to agreement with the leader,there was a deficit which
the committee could not meet and the principle of paying by
voluntary contributions, he feared, would have to be abandoned.
The question was referred to the deacons and music committee.

January 14th. the death of Brother Cull is here recorded and
a reference may be made to the fact that his godly life was a
worthy example for emulation. He, for twenty years, was a
faithful caretaker at the College here and by economy was en-
abled to give liberally to this church towards its support for
over 30 years, and even on his death bed he remembered the

institutions which were entwined around his heart and left small contributions to this church, the Grande Ligne Mission, the Home and Foreign Mission Societies and the balance of his little earnings to a friend.

January 20th, the deacons' report recommended that the church assume the payment of the salary of Miss McDowell and continue Miss Griffith's services for the present, and that a tea meeting be held at an early date to provide funds for the deficit referred to by the committee.—Report adopted and matter referred to the ladies, committee on church work.

January 27th, the ladies' committee reported favorably of the suggestion of a tea meeting and asked for a committee of brethren to assist in the undertaking.—Report adopted and a committee appointed.

January 29th, the death of our dear brother, W. H. Huston, is here recorded. He had been a member of this church only 2 or 3 years but his genial manner and Christ-like disposition for doing good endeared him to all who knew him. His desire to make the College a success in training "his boys for life-work" so largely prevailed that it might be truly said that "he died of over work." That it was a denominational loss was exemplified by the large attendance from all over the land at the memorial services held at the College prior to committing his remains to its last resting place in the Baptist cemetery in this town. Thus was added the last of a large number of honored teachers of that school who gave their lives to the cause they espoused for Christ's sake.

While referring to this subject it should be stated that the successor to Brother Huston in the principalship of the College is our esteemed brother, Joseph I Bates, whose faithful work and experience for 20 years were duly appreciated by the governors of McMaster University in the appointment made.

February 17th, in the absence of the pastor Brother Halliburton occupied the chair.

Brother McKee reported progress in reference to the tea meeting, also read the treasurer's report for the quarter.

The recommendation of the deacons to appoint Mr. T. A. Mc-Cleneghan choir leader was confirmed

It was resolved that two more deacons be appointed at the next regular meeting.

March 16th. Regular monthly meeting. The treasurer reported the proceeds of the teameeting to be $110.

Brethren J. I. Bates and T. C. Mayberry were elected deacons in the usual manner.

R. W. Sawtell reported that after long and serious consideration he had attempted the proposed history of the church and now suggested that a social be held on the seventieth anniversary of the organization of the church, April 22nd, and that part of the programme be the reading of portions of said history for the criticism of the church with a view to its publication.

This was adopted and a committee appointed to carry out the arrangement.

April 6th, special church meeting according to notice. Bro. Beardsall introduced the question of the method of contributing to all denominational objects. After a long discussion on a resolution to raise everything by the envelope plan it was laid upon the table, and the following appointed to consider the matter and bring in a report, viz: R. G. Sawtell, Karn, Beardsall, Dickson, Mayberry and Bates.

April 22nd, 1892, a social was held on this seventieth anniversary when a large number was present. The programme consisted of singing and the reading of the introductory chapters of the history of the church by the writer. After the recess Brother McKechnie moved, seconded by Brother Beardsall that Brother Sawtell be urged to proceed with the history to the present time and that the church assume the publication of the same. The resolution was passed and thus endeth the record to date.

It might be added in conclusion that in no period in the history of the church has it manifested greater zeal for the salvation of souls, greater liberality in giving or greater unity in all departments of church work.

The church is permeated with the Mission spirit. How could it be otherwise, with the continued influence of such men as Father Bates, Dr. Fyfe, John McLaurin, A. V. Timpany and the Bates family, and others who have gone out from this church to the Foreign field?

The greatest harmony prevails with the Oxford street off spring to which there has been dismissed nearly eighty of our actual members. This, however, has been one of the events "that scattereth yet increaseth," for our membership is nearly as large as before. Our gifts to the treasury are yearly increasing and another increase of two hundred dollars has been made to our pastor's salary. For all these and the unenumerated blessings we ascribe to the "God of all grace," glory; honor and grateful adoration.

THE END

www.ingramcontent.com/pod-product-compliance
Lightning Source LLC
Chambersburg PA
CBHW030619270326
41927CB00007B/1243